JOHN DEERE

Hobby Farm

How to Create and Maintain
Your Hobby Farm or Great Estate

Creative Publishing
international

MINNEAPOLIS, MINNESOTA
www.creativepub.com

Creative Publishing
international

Copyright © 2009
Creative Publishing international, Inc.
400 First Avenue North, Suite 300
Minneapolis, Minnesota 55401
1-800-328-3895
www.creativepub.com
All rights reserved

Printed in Singapore
10 9 8 7 6 5 4 3 2 1

Due to differing conditions, materials, and skill levels, the publisher and various manufacturers disclaim any liability for unsatisfactory results or injury due to improper use of tools, materials, or information in this publication.

ISBN-13: 978-1-58923-364-5
ISBN-10: 1-58923-364-6
Library of Congress Cataloging-in-Publication Data

Hampshire, Kristen.
  Hobby farm : how to create and maintain your hobby farm or great estate / Kristen Hampshire.
     p. cm.
  At head of title: Branded by John Deere.
  Summary: "Provides information and instructions for those who own, or dream of owning, a hobby farm or a large estate of 2 to 40 acres"--Provided by publisher.
  ISBN-13: 978-1-58923-364-5 (soft cover)
  ISBN-10: 1-58923-364-6 (soft cover)
  1. Farm management. 2. Farms, Small. I. Title. II. Title: How to create and maintain your hobby farm or great estate.

S561.H224 2008
630--dc22

2008034556

President/CEO: Ken Fund
VP for Sales & Marketing: Kevin Hamric

Publisher: Bryan Trandem
Managing Editor: Tracy Stanley
Senior Editor: Mark Johanson
Editor: Jennifer Gehlhar
Author: Kristen Hampshire

Creative Director: Michele Lanci-Altomare
Senior Design Managers: Jon Simpson, Brad Springer
Design Manager: James Kegley

Lead Photographer: Steve Galvin
Photo Coordinator: Joanne Wawra
Shop Manager: Bryan McLain
Shop Assistant: Cesar Fernandez Rodriguez

Production Managers: Linda Halls, Laura Hokkanen

Cover Design: Val Escher
Page Layout Artist: Val Escher
Photographer: Joel Schnell
Shop Help: Charlie Boldt

Contents

A Hobby Farm of Your Own

Land gives us breathing room—big, blue sky, rolling hay fields, endless gardens and pastures dotted with animals, a yard large enough for a riding mower, at least. Land provides us with a connection to something richer, more natural. Beyond the bustling, high-speed city chase there is land. And on it, croaking frogs welcome spring and delicate fox footprints in the snow remind us that we must share this space.

The promise of vine-ripe tomatoes and farm-fresh eggs, of canned fruit preserves from your own orchard and fresh butter with homemade bread— these images appeal to the inner romantic in us and cause a yearning for a return to our roots.

Land rewards our hard work with its beauty. Its gifts are simple pleasures like fresh-cut flowers. So the decision to expand our horizons and capture more of this space, this dream, piques a keen interest in living on an acre, or several more.

Wide-Open Spaces

For some, a country lifestyle starts as a weekend adventure. Maybe the family rents a vacation home to expose children to nature or to take long hikes and enjoy peace and quiet. A businessman might invest in a second residence on rural property—an escape from the rat race and a place marker for where he plans to spend retirement. Other land lovers grew up in rural areas and want to return. This is where they belong. More recently, there is the appeal of rebelling against a creeping suburbia and staking a claim far out into the country. And as organic foods and sustainable ideals capture interest within the mainstream, a farm is the ultimate way to go green.

But mostly, those who dream of owning more than a ¼-acre city plot have plans for animals, rich gardens, orchards, maybe some bees, and a few chickens. They have cruised by idyllic farms during Sunday drives and gaped at rustic barns and a landscape that delivers a sense of calm. (The farm life, mind you, is never simple and not always that calm.) For all of these reasons, opinions of the country lifestyle have chnaged for the positive.

Large Tract Terminology

Big Backyard: ½ to 3 acres of land surrounding residence.

Great Estate: 3 or more acres of land surrounding residence and consumed primarily by landscape and gardening.

Hobby Farm: Up to 80 acres; landowners produce some income from the land—from hay, vegetables, eggs, or other commodities—but the farm is not their primary source of income.

A PROUD, RED BARN, which many of us associate as a symbol of country life, appears to stand watch over the fields.

A FARM FOR SOME PEOPLE means enough land to grow an elaborate garden and use a riding mower. For others, a farm wouldn't be a farm without animals.

Hobby Farm Profile: Seven Pines

Michael White is former mayor of Cleveland, Ohio, and now an alpaca farmer in Newcomerstown, Ohio, which is two hours southeast of the city he governed for 12 years. He read about alpacas in an in-flight magazine during a business trip. Intrigued by their curious eyes and the sheer beauty of these animals, he began to research the rural lifestyle.

He and his wife, JoAnn, dedicated vacations to alpaca farm tours and studied the business before starting Seven Pines Alpacas. Still, he admits there was a learning curve. "Nothing prepares you for the day a truck pulls up and two alpacas get out," he says, laughing.

"I had to be resourceful," he relates. "If you had a problem in the city, you called someone. You don't call people here. You figure it out." He did have help from generous neighbors, who welcomed the couple to their new community.

Now in its fourth generation of alpacas, Seven Pines is more than a country getaway for the Whites. Raising alpacas is a passion and a business. "Every day it's something new," White says, admitting that he is a "serial mountain climber," always looking for the next challenge. "We're dealing with animals while someone else may deal with widgets, but the technology and information is equally sophisticated."

The New Farm

The word "farm" is a bit misleading in the context of many landowners' intentions for their property. Farms suggest a distinct image of 100-plus acres, probably with a silo and definitely home to crops and cows. But today's hobby farmers may own just a few acres. In fact, many large farms have been parceled into more manageable plots that appeal to city buyers who don't plan to earn their living from the land. The crops and cows and silo—that's all just for fun.

Another distinction in today's farm is property location. The land might be close to urban centers, but just far enough away to be considered the country. There are large estates available in exurbs, and with a few acres you can share the land with some horses. The activities a hobby farmer pursues on the property may be limited to growing grapes or lavender, maybe caring for a milking goat; or pursuits can become more involved with raising a herd of sheep or planting hay and forage crops to feed farm animals.

Ultimately, the defining quality of a hobby farmer is what the land means to his or her livelihood. A hobbyist generates most income from off-farm activity and does not employ full-time labor. A hobby farmer will spend money on the land rather than focus on ways to reap financial rewards from it. Writers, consultants, and small business owners of all kinds discover that an Internet connection is enough to sustain their home-based operations while they gain inspiration and energy from their country lifestyles. They're making a living off their land, but not in the sense that yesterday's farmers did. The animals, gardens, and crops are for play. The land is a big backyard.

Hobby farmers embrace a different pace of life—and by no means a slower one. The land demands constant time and attention, as do animals, crops, flowers, and all other living inhabitants of your country space. The work required to maintain a hobby farm or great estate is fulfilling for those who are looking for tangible rewards for their labor: fresh vegetables, a tidy barnful of happy animals, rolling acres of beautiful land. None of these results come without nurturing. Still, those who choose to move out of the city today do not give up modern conveniences. In many ways, hobby farmers will attest that they get the best of both worlds.

Hobby Farms are Growing

The U.S. Department of Agriculture expects that the rise of lifestyle, or hobby, farms will reverse the shrinking farm trend. Hobby farms are growing 2 percent a year and now account for half of all farms. At the same time, the population of rural counties has increased 12 percent since 1990, the first gain in such areas since the Depression. The same trend is evident in other countries like England. According to the Royal Institution of Chartered Surveyors, nearly half of all farms sold in 2002 were purchased by non-farmers. These landowners seek 20 to 60 acres of land—more than a garden, but not a full-fledged farm.

There is a dual shift where a population of individuals are choosing urban centers rather than settling in suburbia. At the same time, folks are stretching boundaries beyond the burbs to outlying counties so they can purchase a few acres where life seems more relaxed.

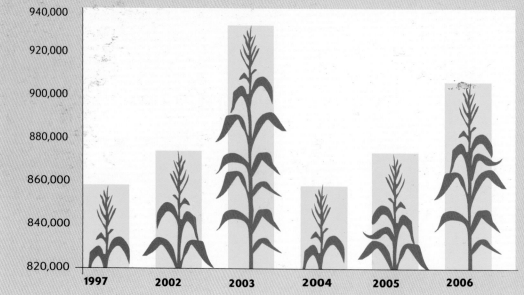

Source: U.S. Department of Agriculture

AN EXPANSIVE BACKYARD can feel like a farm at times, and there are some similarities. You can dedicate a large yard to gardens or even, depending on your local zoning laws, raise a few small animals.

SOME LANDOWNERS seek out acreage to provide a home for their animals. On this horse farm, the animals are a priority and the land a necessity to house them.

Sizing Up the Land

What one person considers a farm, another person calls a big backyard. For an urban dweller who has spent a lifetime living in the core of a major metropolitan center, a 1-acre plot in exurbia may seem like the boondocks. That's country. But those who grew up in rural environments or have been mowing generous backyards for some time, approach the subject of land size with a completely different idea in mind. "Farm" means property with a barn, animals that graze, a sampling of crops, and neighbors at least ½ mile away. That's land.

Regardless of the land's acreage or location, every landowner shares a sense of pride in his or her very own plot of nature. Each property is the product of a dream, hard work, and a commitment to creating something meaningful. That package comes in many different sizes.

Pushing City Limits

As crowded inner-ring suburbs trickle into exurbs and then into lightly developed farmland, the backyards get bigger and the homes are spaced farther apart. These neighborhoods boast plots of at least 1 acre, with plenty of room for a bountiful vegetable garden, a pond, and some breathing room from traffic jams and commercial zones. These big backyards aren't minifarms, and you wouldn't call such a neighborhood "the country." But the concept of owning more land, working the land, and enjoying the land is no different here. Exurban properties require more maintenance and larger equipment. The property presents a healthy challenge for owners who decide to upgrade from their city plots.

DAPHNE BORDEN OF PAYNTER FARM collects the last of her summer's bounty and prepares her garden for winter.

Lifestyle Farms

For many, animals represent the most compelling appeal to country life. Perhaps you've dreamed of owning horses or caring for a small flock of sheep. Properties that allow for such pursuits are usually located in rural communities, though sometimes close enough to a city for commuting to work. Minifarms provide enough space for an elaborate garden, a barn with animals, and certainly chickens. Regular maintenance keeps a whole family busy, but minifarm property is manageable and the right size for hobbyists.

THIS SMALL FLOCK of curious sheep prefer to roam in a huddle.

Ruralpolitan Living

Those who choose land in a "ruralpolitan" area do not have to sacrifice convenience. Sure, the grocery store may be 15 miles away, and the town won't offer restaurant choices or a robust retail environment. But these communities are strongly influenced by neighboring metropolitan or resort areas, which are usually within two hours' driving distance. Ruralpolitan areas are wired with technology, catering to telecommuters and entrepreneurs with home-based businesses. Still, they are country. Land is generous, and some folks are "agripreneurs" who make a living from the land. Many more people are taking advantage of affordable property in these areas for a change of lifestyle or a place to vacation.

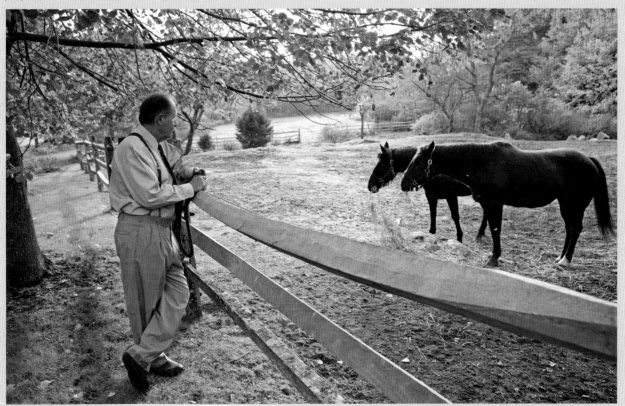

BOB BORDEN COMMUTES FROM PAYNTER FARM to downtown Boston several days a week. Coming home to a peaceful environment is truly an escape for him.

LANDOWNERS WITH AMPLE ACREAGE may dedicate portions of their land for growing vegetables, raising animals, and recreation.

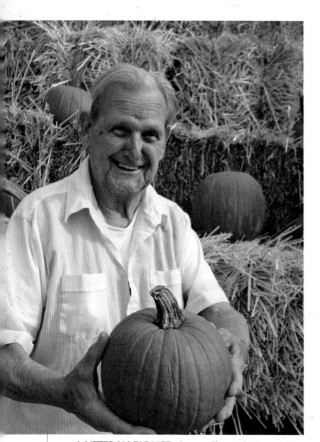

A VETERAN FARMER shows off a perfect pumpkin.

PEACE AND QUIET IN THE COUNTRY—the freedom to "unplug" from modern hassles appeals to some landowners who seek property off the grid.

A CUTTING GARDEN will yield a bounty of beautiful bouquets for the home—but growing flowers is just as much work as producing fresh vegetables.

Room to Breathe

A property that is 50 acres may include woods for hunting, a yard where children play, orchards, pastures, gardens, and more. A water source, whether a stream or pond, is always an attractive feature. With so much space, a land plan is critical—and so is time. A hobby farm isn't a summer landscape project. It's a constant work in progress that involves cooperation with Mother Nature and patience. Those who pore their soul into the land can imagine no other life.

Off the Grid

Homesteading is a lot more comfortable today and quite a departure from the pioneer days. If building a house from straw bales, roofing it with solar panels, and trading the television satellite for a wind turbine is your idea of taking to the land, technology is on your side. Future off-the-grid dwellers may power their homes with fuel cells that convert hydrogen into electricity. The draw for those who choose this organic approach is sustainability—learning to make use of the land and its bounty, and unplugging from the rat race.

SOLAR PANELS can reduce energy expenses and are ideal for south-facing roof surfaces. Keep in mind, depending on your region and the season, you may not be able to rely on solar heat entirely.

Farm Pursuits

Your land is a canvas, and though it may already contain outlines and etchings, such as an existing hay pasture or a century-old barn, you can erase and redraw, reinvent, and start from scratch. There are some elements you must work with, including topography, soil content, water quality, existing infrastructure, and zoning restrictions. Sun exposure and wind patterns will also dictate land use. Before you purchase property, talk to the current landowner and neighbors about the land. Find out what grows and what doesn't. Learn the zoning restrictions.

Depending on the size of your property, you can raise a vegetable garden or plant corn or soybeans. You may keep a chicken coop, or if your neighbors are far enough away to avoid the "exhaust," you can tend to pigs. With a few acres and a barn, horses are a possibility; add several more acres for a sizable flock of sheep to roam. Be sure to check with your local municipality for laws regulating land use for animals. You may also want to check with animal awareness groups to best determine the space requirements and shelter requirements for your livestock; often these groups recommend the best living conditions for animals above and beyond the base needs required by local law (see Resources section).

You'll find out just how handy you are as you develop hobbies that are byproducts of the vegetables and animals you raise: canning vegetables, making preserves, hand spinning fleece into yarn, woodworking, and creating pottery.

WITH BOUNTY TO SPARE, hobby farmers may try their luck at agripreneurship and sell produce at local farmers markets like this one.

THE MESH FENCE will prevent critters from destroying the bounty.

Crops

Sustainability is a driver for landowners who raise crops and animals. Waste helps fertilize gardens and fields, and leftover vegetables or crops like hay will feed sheep, horses, goats, or cows. Also, there is nothing like the sweet taste of corn right from the field or the satisfaction of digging potatoes, beets, and carrots from the soil you mended and tilled yourself. You can cross produce off your grocery list if you grow your own. As boutique vegetables and heirloom varieties grow in popularity, often emerging as ingredients chefs demand for local upscale restaurants and local markets, some hobby farmers are testing these specialty crops in hopes of marketing the goods for a higher profit—and many are succeeding.

Gardens

Growing fresh produce and flowers often is an instant temptation for new landowners. Gardening is an opportunity to play in the dirt. You learn what the land requires in order for it to serve as an inviting bed for seedlings, as well as how to manage pests and weather extremes. Gardens are especially attractive to new landowners who buy property in the outskirts of suburbia. An exurban property is an opportunity to expand their former city-scaled garden and move beyond raised beds and container plantings.

The great thing about gardens is that they don't require a tremendous amount of space. You can till a plot on your property and plant rows of vegetables; or you can establish raised beds, which can accommodate drainage issues your land may present. But no matter the size of your land, start small. Find out which plants flourish, then grow your garden.

IF THE CROP IS BOUNTIFUL, you may preserve the produce by canning it or making fresh jams so you're able to enjoy the tastes of summer all year long.

FRESHLY SHORN WOOL is a renewable animal product, and there are many other valuable resources, such as meat and eggs, that raising animals can provide.

THERE'S REASON for the name "hog-right fence." Curious pigs will wander without a well-built barrier.

Animals

What's a farm without the animals: chickens, pigs, goats, sheep, cows, some horses to ride? Depending on how much room you have to house animals, you may grow your kingdom to include a cast of farm characters. For many landowners, animals are just that: companions, doted-after pets. But before you adopt a whole crew, be realistic about the resources you'll need to provide: shelter, grazing space (for some), food, veterinarian care. Chickens are ideal for most land sizes, and you can keep a single goat as a "lawnmower" for your yard. Horses are happy with a few acres and a suitable barn. As you grow a herd of sheep or cows, be sure your pastures allow room for them to roam freely. Again, be sure to check local regulations on required land size for the type and number of animals you plan to invite onto your property. Also check with local animal awareness groups for your specific type of animal to determine the ideal amount of space, shelter, grass types, etc. This information at times differs from the base requirements set forth by local laws.

PIGS ARE POPULAR 4-H projects for kids.

HORSES PROVIDE COMPANIONSHIP **and recreation.**

Recreation

Necessity is a great motivator. You need a barn, so you learn carpentry skills. You have a storeroom of fleeces from shorn sheep, so you teach yourself how to spin yarn to make good use of the wool. You take up canning and experiment with new recipes as your harvest improves. You discover how to attract butterflies to your garden and get to know the birds that make a flight path through your property. The simple pleasures of country life are fulfilling, and they satisfy the desire to work with our hands.

RELAXING VISTAS, SUNSHINE, AND CLEAN AIR are compelling lures for city folk who are tired of being mired in traffic, noise, and pollution.

Is This the One?

Searching for farmland involves a completely different set of variables than hunting for real estate in the suburbs. For one, the farmhouse is largely an accessory to the package. More important are the less romantic features: terrain, access roads, water, septic systems, drainage, deeds, and easements. Of course, it's easy to get wrapped up in the vast curb appeal that is farmland. We're talking endless pastures, big, blue sky, a horse barn, the works. Shopping is the fun part: navigating scenic country roads on a Sunday in search of that perfect plot of land. But take it slow. Remember, you're marrying your goals with a spot of land that must accommodate them.

Enlist a realtor with local expertise to help you through the process (see page 22). As you consider various farm communities and exurban areas, talk to people who live there. Subscribe to local newspapers, eat at local lunch counters, shop at the hardware store. In short, get a feel for the area.

Someone with experience in rural real estate will be on the lookout for warning signs that a property has flooding problems, water-quality issues, accessibility challenges, or other qualities that could make your job as a landowner more difficult. As you look for land, remember that the property is a canvas you can change by grading, building roads, adding landscape, planting crops—but you can only do so much. Some terrain isn't meant for planting, and you'll struggle to clear the thistle and invasive brush and convert the land to fertile soil. All of this can be done, but consider first the amount of work you want to put into the land to get it into shape. You can buy raw land with no house, no road, no nothing. Or you can acquire a property that is already "in business," so to speak. Discuss these options with your realtor.

LOCATING AND PURCHASING the land for your hobby farm or great estate requires an extensive, if not exhaustive, amount of legwork and thought.

The Call of the Alpacas

When they decided to buy a hobby farm, about the only thing Michael and Joanne White knew for sure was that they wanted to raise alpacas.

Michael White didn't know a lot about alpacas at the time, but he knew the first step was to find land. He and his wife planned to commute to their property the first couple of years and use the place as a weekend getaway until White finished his final term as mayor of Cleveland. Then, they would move and Seven Pines Alpacas would be a full-time pursuit.

What resulted was a much longer commute and a lot more land than they had expected to purchase: 45 acres of hilly, rough canvas that looked like Jurassic Park overrun with invasive multiflora. There was no driveway, no house, no pond, and the property was 100 miles from home in Cleveland. But their purchase was, by no means, a compromise.

"We liked the fact that it was quiet; we had our own little world," White says. "We appreciate all of the hills—the beauty. A wise person once said that progress is always about seeing the apple in the seed. We were standing in the seed, we just had to see the apple."

Today, Michael reflects on all of the exhausting farm shopping, the meetings with the land agent to discuss properties for sale, the trips out to visit land, and all of the dead ends. Keeping an open mind was critical, but so was enlisting a professional. He and his wife had to understand their goals for the property so they could ensure the land would accommodate alpacas and a horse rescue foundation.

SEVEN PINES ALPACAS owner Michael White transitioned from public office to a farm, where he and wife JoAnn raise and sell alpacas and shelter rescued horses.

The Location

When farm shopping, the first decision you need to make concerns location. Yes, location, location . . . this factor can make or break your happiness on a farm. By this point, you've done some soul searching and have a grasp on whether your family is enthusiastic about a move to a rural community, or if a couple of acres in an exurban environment not too far away from the nearest shopping center is more suitable. How close must you be to cultural activities, a big city, or places to shop and eat out? If none of these considerations matter, then location may take you away from civilization as you have known it. On the farm, you will find new sources of entertainment in the animals, gardening, and outdoor projects your land requires.

If you have children, think about schools. What is the travel time? Will your children take a bus, and will you have the time to transport them to activities?

Consider health care. Access to health care providers is a major concern in rural communities. Where is the closest hospital? What basic medical needs are provided right in the community? What is the quality of these services?

What about churches, grocery stores, and markets to sell your produce, if you plan to do so? How accessible is the land to major routes and highways? And, as you must ask yourself with each of these items, is this important to you?

If you can, extend your farm shopping adventure through the seasons so you can observe how the land changes and responds to weather. You may decide the hillsides will inhibit your crop aspirations or that a road would be better rerouted because of wind patterns that create unmanageable snow drifts in winter.

WELL WATER is common in the country. The county or state health department can test for contamination.

The Infrastructure

Before you get too excited about the breathtaking vistas on the property, dig into the underlayers. What good is a bucolic backyard if you can't drink the water or flush the toilet without a disaster?

Water—Good, clean water from a reliable source is a must. If you are accustomed to tap water, the rural water scene will introduce a new world of wells, cisterns, irrigation, and flood zones. The property should be equipped with a well (you may share with neighbors) that can provide enough safe water for drinking and watering crops or gardens. Find out how much water your well can provide. Review the Safe Drinking Water Act standards and be sure the seller agrees that the well or cistern is up to par. Also, your home and outbuildings should sit away from riverbanks, creeks, and ponds to avoid risk of flooding.

Drainage—Both vegetable gardens and livestock pens require good drainage. If you visit the property during a dry spell, you may not imagine that pastures turn to muck and the basement floods when it rains. You can access topographic maps from the U. S. Geological Survey or TerraService.net.

Septic System—Find out the age and size of your septic system. If you are moving your family to a home inhabited by a single person who has lived there alone for years, the septic tank may require upgrading or replacement. Septic tanks are sized according to bedroom and plumbing fixtures. You should not purchase a home unless the parcel has passed percolation tests. A percolation test measures the ability of soil to absorb liquid. The test results are used to construct septic systems. The test also reveals the suitability of a site for a private sewage disposal system. Refer to your county extension office for more information.

Utilities—Unless you are living off the grid, you'll want to ask about electricity, natural gas, cable or satellite television, Internet access, and phone services. Depending on the location of a property, some of these services may not be available.

The Elements

The specific features of any property will ultimately attract you to the land. The way pastures tumble over hilly topography and fade into the woods. A back-porch view of an apple orchard where sheep nose around for tart, fallen leftovers. A slow creek, a watercolor sunset, the sound of wind whisking through hay fields. Call it organic curb appeal. When you find "the one," you just know.

But be practical. Review your goals for the land. For instance, if growing crops doesn't matter, neither will poor soil quality. However, you'll dedicate a lot of time and resources to amending sizable pastures that are out of shape for growing corn.

Also consider which elements exist on the property and whether you want to care for them. If there is a large field of hay for feeding livestock but you want nothing to do with large crop farming and you merely plan to raise chickens, maybe that isn't the property for you. While you can groom the land to meet your goals, you don't want to embark on a project that will empty your bank account.

FOR SAFETY AND CONVENIENCE, consider each property's proximity to main byways.

The Fine Print

As with any real estate search, a prime objective is to avoid surprises. We've touched on the basics to keep in mind when searching for property, but a short lesson isn't enough for such a major investment. Seek out a realtor who can help you identify desirable properties that meet your demands and your budget. Partner with someone who knows the area and understands farm life. Ask for someone who specializes in land transactions. And be prepared to wait—the chances are slim that your dream piece of land happens to be on the market just when you're ready to start looking.

As you explore land for sale and find a winner, consult with an attorney and a professional title examiner. Before purchasing any property, review a recorded plat, certified survey map, or the last deed recorded on the parcel. These documents, along with a legal description of the land, can be obtained from the county recorder's office. You can also check your local library for commercially prepared plat books or refer to an assessor's office or the county extension office.

The paperwork ultimately determines what you can build, grow, or raise on your property. There may be zoning restrictions, easements, and deeds that could help or hinder your plan. Read the fine print before you go forward with any land deal.

Ask John Deere

Q: Is it necessary to work with a land agent when searching for property?
A: That depends on the size and cost of the property, how much you are willing to spend, and how familiar you are with the area in which you are looking. Normally, a real estate agent will be able to show farms and large properties for sale. But if you are looking at multimillion dollar properties, it's a good idea to seek out a land agent who specializes in large-scale land transactions.
~Sean Sundberg, product specialist, John Deere

BEFORE YOU SIGN on the dotted line, survey the land and learn about any deeds or easements on your property.

Start your land search online by checking out your local real estate websites. Also browse these comprehensive online listings:

- LandAndFarm.com
- RuralProperty.com
- FarmSeller.com
- UnitedCountry.com

Zoning & Land Use

How the land is zoned will determine whether a subdivision could crop up within eyeshot of your back porch or whether you can raise pigs as you planned. Find out if the area is being rezoned, and keep an eye open for development announcements if you are concerned about a new development disturbing the peace.

Are there building codes that will prevent you from building a barn or adding on a sunroom? Find out what paperwork must be filed before you break ground. Otherwise, learn the hard way like Sean Sundberg, a product specialist for John Deere, who found out he needed approval to build a deck on his rural Wisconsin property when the tax man paid a visit. "I was in the country, so I didn't think I had to ask anyone first," he says. "I had to go backward through the channels and prove that the footings for the deck were as deep as they were stipulated in the county code. I paid a couple of fines."

Land use regulations may prevent you from keeping certain animals on the property. Don't buy the animals before the farm, and be sure there aren't restrictions on what breeds can roam on the land.

Easements

Essentially, an easement gives another party the right to use your property or portions of it. For example, if the utility company has an easement on a portion of your land and decides to run power lines through your pasture, there's nothing you can do about it (other than move your livestock to a different area of the farm). Or, the county may have an easement on a portion of your property to build connecting roads. Easements can exist on a property for decades without being used, but you should know whether they exist and how this could affect your land. Also find out if your deed contains reservations for minerals or oil, for example.

Sealing the Deal

In a property transaction, the deed is a document that confirms the property transfer. In a quitclaim deed, the seller no longer has interest or claim to the property. A warranty deed comes with a written guarantee from the seller that he or she has the right to sell the property and will work to clear up any problems that should arise after the sale. The seller can't walk away from responsibilities, nor can he or she interpret this warranty as a right to force you off the land in any way. A warranty deed provides more protection for the buyer. In a deed of trust, the real property is given as security for the mortgage debt. A third-party trustee, such as a bank or lender, holds the deed until the loan is paid in full.

Regardless of the type of deed, involve an attorney during the closing process. By then, you will have investigated the property survey, parcel description, building codes, zoning restrictions, and easements and gathered details on water quality and septic systems—the works. Remember, the goal is to avoid surprises. A realtor or attorney can make sure that nothing leaks into the fine print that could prevent you from fulfilling your goals for the land.

Farm Organization

Keep a farm folder for each property that interests you. Start your information-gathering process by obtaining a parcel description from the county recorder's office. Compare this description with what you see on the land. Use this document as a reference as you consult with government offices about zoning, septic systems, and other infrastructure and codes that pertain to the property.

CHAPTER **2**

Improving the Land

Whether or not your property is equipped with the infrastructure necessary to raise animals and vegetables and to promote drainage and protect your equipment, there are plenty of projects that will improve your land and truly make it your own. Some of these improvements are essential. If you keep goats, you can't live without good, strong fencing. The same is true for pigs. You also must have an access road and a driveway. Perhaps windbreaks or culverts are also in order.

You won't complete these improvements in a summer's time. This isn't a suburban landscape project. So begin by putting your ideas on paper, and create a phase plan that prioritizes items on your list. This section helps you get started.

The Land Plan

You're dealing with a landscape project of an entirely different scale than before. This is no backyard renovation. Forget the weekend warrior idea. Instead, think of your land as a model you will shape over time. Your plan is a long-term work in progress. Don't rush it.

Digest the scope of your land plan by breaking projects down into realistic portions. You can manage building a small landscape pond in a weekend, but a large farm pond could take weeks. Clearing land can take years and may be an ongoing process, and hobby farmers will tell you that fencing is a never-ending task of installation and repair.

Approach your land plan as though you are entering into a marriage. Problems will crop up and demand immediate attention. The plan will evolve over time. No matter how hard you try, your land will never be perfect. But you'll love it anyway.

WELSH MOUNTAIN PONIES, mares and foals, exercise in a fenced pasture. Over time, you will complete projects such as fences to improve your land and its functionality.

Tuning in at Turning Point Farm

When Albert and Cheryl Laufer purchased their 135-acre farm in Newbury, Ohio, they had a good year of planning before they moved there full-time.

"We allowed time to watch what happened during different seasons," says Albert Laufer. He walked through the 80 acres of woods to test potential routes for their future driveway. When they purchased the farm, there were pastures in place and a farm road that cut through the fields. Laufer knew he would need to reconstruct a dam that crossed wetlands and plot where to build the barn, road, and house.

"We watched the direction of the wind, how the sun moved throughout the year, and then we tried to use the sun to our advantage and conquer the wind problems," he describes. With that knowledge, the Laufers decided to build their barn facing east-west rather than windy north-south. The driveway winds through a wooded portion of their lot, sparing important trees and avoiding lowlands prone to flooding.

"All this was part of the game plan," Laufer relates.

ALBERT AND CHERYL LAUFER observed their farmland patiently for a full year before making any decisions on improving the land.

Take Inventory

Watch, listen, and take note of your property's special characteristics: Which direction does the wind blow? Where does the sunlight fall? Which native plants grow well, and where? Are there signs of erosion or other changes in the topography of the land? Do you notice vulnerable areas that may require stabilization?

Land surveys and the terrain map collected during the farm shopping process will help you learn the story of your land. But there is no replacement for taking the time to get to know your land firsthand during every season.

First, address the land plan. This involves assessing areas of your property that could present problems and then listing those trouble spots. Also answer some basic questions: How do weather conditions affect your prop-

erty? Will you struggle with snow drifts? Which places, if any, are prone to flooding during the wet season? Finally, address what is missing from the land. Do you need or want to build roads, pathways, a barn, fencing, or outbuildings for storage? What kinds of aesthetic features do you desire?

Use this list to create a bubble diagram that maps low-lying areas prone to flooding and windy zones. Note which zones are most conducive to planting. Are there spaces overtaken by invasive plants that require clearing? Don't worry, your drawing does not need to be a masterpiece. Just get these concepts on paper so you can better visualize how your improvement projects will take shape on the land.

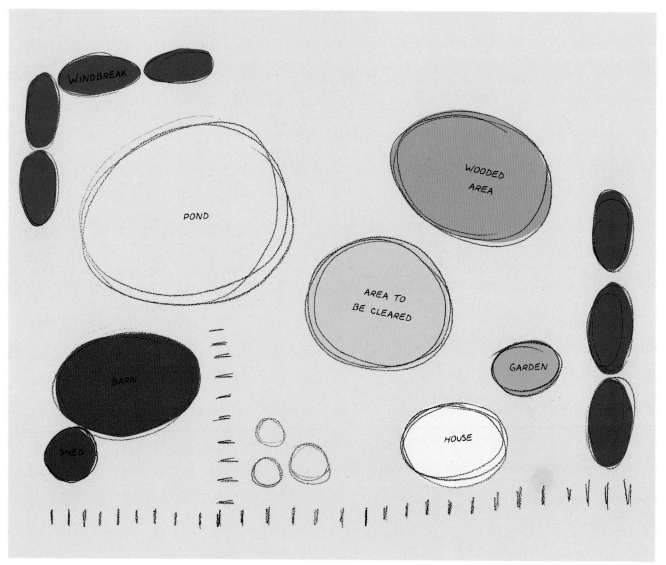

SKETCH YOUR PLAN for the land so you can visualize how each project fits into the big picture.

Draw Bubble Plans

MAKE A TRACING OF YOUR SITE MAP that includes the property boundaries and any structures and features that will be included in your new landscape.

EXPERIMENT WITH LAYOUTS for your landscape by drawing several different bubble plans. Use smooth, flowing lines for the boundaries of each space.

SELECT THE BUBBLE PLAN THAT BEST SUITS YOUR NEEDS and preferences. Redraw it carefully and label the various living spaces according to their purpose.

Prioritize and Budget

As you develop a plan for your land, evaluate the necessity of the project, the skills and equipment required to complete each project, and the estimated cost. Decide what you can feasibly do by yourself and which tasks you'll need to contract out to professionals. Land clearing can take five years with a single person performing manual labor and a flock of sheep to do the mowing. Or, you can contract a company with heavy-duty equipment to clear the land in a couple of months. Your budget will dictate this.

Some questions to ask as you prioritize your projects include:

- **Is this project essential to our infrastructure? Can the farm function without it?**
- **Can we complete the project ourselves?**
- **What type of equipment do we need? Do we own these tools, or can we affordably rent the equipment?**
- **Can all or parts of the project be contracted out to a professional at an affordable rate?**

Not all properties will require large-scale improvements. If the thought of cutting through a sea of thistle or erecting a fence is enough to send you packing back to the big-city high-rise condo, then consider properties that aren't so labor intensive. Many exurban landscapes require a riding mower for maintenance, and the projects you pursue are simply bigger versions of what you find on suburban lots. The extent of the improvements necessary to convert the land into the home of your dreams should weigh heavily into your initial purchase decision.

Clearing Land

Nuisance trees, invasive plants, and thorny groundcovers latch on to your land and form a vegetative brigade that sends a clear message to keep out. They're stubborn. But if you want to dedicate land for crops, a pasture, or a big backyard, you need to clear the way.

Left unrestrained, thistle, weeds, trees, and overgrowth will inevitably take over any piece of property. If your lot is a sea of thorny brush or is entirely wooded, you must clear portions of it to make room for your home and a yard, at the very least. The question is how do you get rid of the mess?

There are options. You can hire an excavator, logger, or someone with heavy-duty bulldozing equipment to manage the job. This is a costly solution. If you are not in a hurry, you may decide to clear the land yourself using a combination of manual labor and rental equipment (like a backhoe or skid loader) to topple, remove, pile, and clear vegetative debris, including trees. Most likely, you'll clear some of the land yourself and rely on hired help to manage certain tasks, such as removing large trees.

But before you can decide what is feasible to manage solo, return to your land plan and approach this project with a distinct understanding of what lies beneath all that brush.

Scope Out the Territory

Your first task is to walk your property to survey the land on foot. So put on a pair of canvas pants, some sturdy gloves, and safety goggles, and set out. Bring along a brush cutter or machete to slice through vegetative tangles. Explore the area and get a feel for the topography. Take photos and make notes.

Depending on the type of vegetation that is consuming your land, your manpower may not be enough to cut through the mass. There are different techniques for clearing junk brush and mature trees.

Before you attempt to alter the topography of your land, consider the time and equipment required to do the job. Clearing land is no easy task. It's labor intensive, and certainly not a project you can complete during a weekend. For instance, land owners who rely on grazing sheep or goats to chew away brush may wait nearly a decade before the land is in condition to use. The scope of your project—whether your clearing job means removing a few trees, or excavating thistle from several acres—will dictate which clearing method is appropriate. Following are some options.

LAND CLEANUP is a daunting but necessary task that requires heavy-duty equipment like this tractor and bucket attachment.

Invasive Groundcover

Fields inundated with a mess of invasive, thorny brush can be cleared completely for crops, a tree farm, vineyard, or lawn. Clear-cutting involves removing all nuisance trees and vegetation—think of it as wiping the land clean. You'll probably amend soil, seed, and grow grass or pasture when you're done. Keep in mind, screening and woodlands are equally important to a country setting. Always clear-cut with a purpose.

You can cut back invasive brush by hand using a root talon or weed wrench. If you own a brush hog (also called a Bush Hog after the equipment's brand name) or a rotary mower attachment for rough cutting, you can whack thistle. But this machine will only work if the vegetative growth is not too tall or excessively tangled.

You may use a backhoe to topple and dislodge roots from the soil, then to lift out and gather extensive brush in a pile. With a permit, some counties allow you to burn brush during certain times of the day. Check into this first by contacting your local extension service. You may need to remove leftover stumps with a skid steer loader. This machine can also grade land, smooth out areas where stumps and roots left holes, and push material around as you create piles.

BRUSH-CRASHING is the only way to know what mysteries and challenges reside on your property behind the masses of branches and bramble. Dress for protection and, if you haven't explored the property, enlist a companion just in case.

Wooded Lots

If your property is a virtual forest, removing trees is essential for planting a garden or creating a small roaming area for animals. Before dozing through the space, find out whether you can sell the lumber. The firewood you gain from logging—and, in essence, clearing your land—can provide a revenue source to apply toward the clearing project or other improvements.

A logging company can cut down trees, drag them from the woods, and transport them to a wood yard for sale. For substantial wood-clearing projects, consider checking with a forestry consultant for an estimate of the total worth of the timber on your property. Collect bids from logging companies. Your reward is clear land with leftover stumps and perhaps a bit of leftover brush. This can be dealt with by using a skid steer loader or a backhoe with attachments, including a front-end loader rake and forks for lifting and moving piles.

Land Invaders

THESE INVASIVE PLANTS can really cause a problem if you are trying to maintain clear land.

Buckthorn

Multiflora/Wild Rose (hip)

Multiflora/Wild Rose (bloom)

Briar

Thistle

Bittersweet

Purple Loosestrife

Poison Ivy

LAND CLEARING can take as little time as months, or as long as years.

Topple, Uproot, Remove

You can clear wooded lots with trees that are 4 inches (10.2 cm) in diameter or less with the help of a backhoe. A backhoe with a bucket attachment unearths tree roots and accomplishes moving and clearing tasks. However, you should never remove a tree that is too large for you to manage. It's best to consult with a tree expert if you are uncertain.

How to Remove a Small Tree with a Backhoe

- Backhoe
- Attachments: 4-in-1 bucket
- Additional attachments for moving piles and cleanup: front-end loader rake, forks with large tines (preferably 40" [101.6 cm] or larger)

1. Slice the roots. You must slice through larger tree roots to loosen the trunk before you can effectively remove the tree. Do so by positioning the bucket on the ground to one side of the trunk, 1 or 2 ft. (30.5 to 61 cm) away from the base. Sink the bucket at least 1 ft. (30.5 cm) into the ground. Curl the bucket inward and back toward the machine. Repeat on the other side of the trunk, if necessary.

2. Topple the tree. With the backhoe bucket curled under, use the bucket base to topple the tree away from the machine.

3. Remove the root ball. Use the bucket to pivot the tree at a 45° angle away from the machine so the trunk does not obstruct access to the root ball. Curl the bucket under the root ball, close the bucket, and lift the tree and root ball from the ground. Shake the root ball so loose soil falls into the leftover hole.

4. Grapple and move the tree. Curl the bucket around the tree trunk and transport it to a pile if you are clearing out multiple small trees. Create a pile with root balls collected at one end, and do not allow separate piles to overlap, as you will complicate the process of collecting the pile with your fork tool. Make piles less than 6 to 8 ft. (1.8 to 2.4 m) tall and no wider than the fork attachment.

NATURE'S LAWN MOWERS AT WORK. Sheep, goats, and other grazing animals are more than happy to assist in the clearing and lawn-keeping chores. If you are maintaining a group of animals, it's important to move them around with some frequency so they do not eat too much of each plant, which inhibits plant growth.

Natural Clearing

Grazing can get the job done if your goal is to manage weeds and pasture growth. Your sheep will maintain the property you worked so hard to clear. Other effective "grazing mowers" include goats and cows. A single goat kept around a house can virtually eliminate regular mowing. Of course, you won't get the striping or evenness from a pet mower, but there is a lot to be said about eliminating a chore from your to-do list. Plus, you can feel good about eliminating the pollution that gas-powered lawn mowers cause.

Before you let animals loose on the land, read up on managed grazing, which prescribes the type of pasture grasses and appropriate grass length for grazing. Shoot for a pasture comprised of 40 percent legumes, such as clover or alfalfa. Don't graze plants that are less than 5 inches (12.7 cm) tall, and allow newly seeded pasture grass to reach 8 inches (20.3 cm) before grazing. The purpose of managed grazing is to strike a balance of mowing your pastures by cud-chewing creatures without stripping the land, which encourages weed growth and prompts erosion problems. Meanwhile, be sure you do not have poisonous plants in your pasture that animals may accidentally eat.

Clearing a View

Before clearing the thistle and briar that consumed most of Paynter Farm, there were few paths Daphne Borden could walk to reach a swale on the salt marshes that surround the property. These marshes collect the high tides from the Atlantic ocean every six hours, offering the property a taste of brine. The farmhouse sits on 13 acres, where sheep and Daphne's favorite horse play in an apple orchard. From the kitchen window, Daphne can watch her animals in the orchard and see the marshes, no more than 300 yards from the house. A split-rail fence divides a modest backyard from the rest of the land. "Before, you couldn't see anything beyond that fence line," she says.

"We had five old apple trees that were just barely making it, and we could tell we had a pasture," Daphne continues, describing the land when she and her husband, Bob, first purchased it. "No one had taken care of it for at least 30 years."

Daphne cleared the land by hand using clippers and a chain saw and a herd of sheep for cleanup. The process took seven years, and the sheep still maintain the clearing. But now, the Bordens enjoy an unobstructed view of the marshland.

PAYNTER FARM has remained protected from development because of the surrounding marshlands.

DEPENDING ON THE PURPOSE OF YOUR ROAD, you may choose to pave it with dirt or gravel. Pavement and blacktop are generally reserved for shorter driveways or parking areas because of the expense.

Building Roads

The land you admire for its distance from the daily hubbub, endless sweet-smelling pastures, enchanting woods, and musical creeks must include a less romantic element if you want to access your property and enjoy it. Roads—good, strong roads that last—are essential infrastructure.

You need access to a main road and, depending on the size of your property, driveways that connect house to barn to field. Perhaps the existing roads on your property are nothing but dirt trails or mowed-down paths. On virgin land, you're probably starting this project from scratch. Don't underestimate the job. A stable, sensible road requires a land plan, soil preparation, and the right materials for the job.

Roads are a definite selling point of property for sale. If you can purchase land with driveway infrastructure already in place, you can save quite a bit of time and money. If you purchase undeveloped land, you may negotiate with the seller to include a road allowance or see whether the owner will consider doing this job for you as part of the deal. However, there are real benefits to building roads yourself. First, you can't be sure that the previous owner did an A-plus job, and you may want to decide for yourself how to direct traffic—that even means your vehicles—through your property. Assuming you'll take on the project yourself, here are some considerations to keep in mind as you plan and build your road.

Material Matters

Ultimately, cost is the deciding factor when choosing material for a road. The longer your road, the more surface area it has, and therefore it carries a steeper price tag, especially if you want a paved surface. You may opt to pave select areas, such as a stretch from your house to the barn or a parking area by your garage.

Gravel: requires less repair; won't heave or crack, making it cost-effective.

Asphalt: better appearance, no dust, ease of snowplowing

Dirt: without proper drainage turns to soup after a downpour, cost-effective and about as back to the basics as you can get.

Gravel is sold by the square yard. First build a base of asphalt or larger rock chunks, then lay down #57 gravel, which is $1/2$ to $3/4$" (1.3 to 1.9 cm), before topping the base with a smaller #47 gravel. It has sharp edges and stays in place. Crushed gravel is less expensive than stone, and it reduces frost heaves, though removing snow from it is difficult.

Stone may shift around more because of its smooth edges, though it effectively drains water. Stone is more attractive than crushed gravel (boosting the price tag).

Road Map

Think of your property as a blank canvas. Now, add topography: hills, wetlands, steep grades, ruts. What lies beneath? Clay soil becomes slippery when wet and requires stabilizing to support roads. Sandy soil erodes easily. To best assess the condition of your land and what you should do to build a long-lasting road, enlist the expertise of a soil conservationist or a county cooperative extension agent to analyze your soil and offer suggestions before excavation.

Next, watch water patterns. Notice where rainwater rushes and where it collects. Find the highlands and the lowlands, and take note of areas that flood. Water is your enemy when building roads. It can cause flooding and puddling, and freeze-thaw cycles eventually cause buckling and dig pits into the surface. Meanwhile, water moving within the soil profile weakens roads, causing them to shift, sink, and flood.

Now imagine a blizzard—snowdrifts and ice. Could you plow through the road? What are the wind patterns? Think about the very worst winter day you have experienced, or a torrential downpour in warmer climates, and how you would navigate the roadway. Plan for the worst.

An excavator can help you determine the best path through your land. You may also want a surveyor to shoot grades. Ideally, roadway grades should not exceed 6 percent.

In many ways, the land dictates how you will get from point A to point B on your property. But you can build up soil, create watersheds, and manage drainage if you know about these conditions before you begin.

A SATELLITE MAP OF YOUR PROPERTY is a great tool for assessing your existing roads and plotting new roads.

Road Construction

Most roadways are 10 to 12 feet wide (3.0 to 3.7 m), though you may require more clearance to accommodate vehicles and equipment. The type of material you choose for the surface ultimately depends on the length of your road and your budget.

Money is well spent on professionals like excavator operators who have the heavy-duty equipment required to haul materials to your property, clear topsoil, tamp a base of broken asphalt, and roll and spread gravel.

However, if all you need is a basic driveway that cuts through a large front yard to the main street, you can accomplish this project yourself by either renting equipment or using a skid steer loader and attachments.

A stable road requires several layers of material. One approach is a base of broken asphalt pieces, a middle layer of larger gravel, and a surface of stone-sized gravel. Roads should crown slightly in the center so water runs off on either side.

Case Study

When Albert and Cheryl Laufer built two roads on their 170-acre property in Newbury, Ohio, gravel was the most economical option. A 2,900 ft. road snakes through woods on their property and cuts through a pasture leading to the main byway. Another 2,200 ft. driveway leads from the barns that house their alpacas to their hillside home. The scope of their project demanded an economical approach. Asphalt or concrete can potentially double the cost of the project. The Laufers first laid 20" (50.8 cm) of broken asphalt pieces as a base. They built their roads in the summertime, so heat melted the asphalt, and an excavator packed it down with a backhoe attachment. Next, the excavator laid down #57 gravel, pieces that are ¹/₂ to ³/₄" (1.3 to 1.9 cm). This was spread and packed down before adding the top layer of smaller #47 gravel.

Gravel (2-4")

Compactible gravel (4-6")

Asphalt (10-20")

CROSS SECTION OF A GRAVEL ROAD. Each layer is laid and compacted. The road should crown in the center to encourage runoff.

To prevent erosion near the roadway where you have stripped topsoil and likely disturbed nearby growth, replant on exposed soil. Trees or shrubs can improve the aesthetics if your road-building project compromised the land.

Drainage Solutions

You can't beat Mother Nature, but you can control the lay of the land by building water courses, water bars, and drainage crossings to encourage water to run away from the road. Water courses are shallow V-shaped carvings on either side of the roadway. Water collects in these Vs rather than puddling on the road. Water bars are small graded ridges that direct water out of ruts and into a planned drainage system. Drainage crossings prevent that small gully or harmless ditch from turning into a rushing river during a heavy rain. (That rushing river will flood your road.) Drainage crossings require a culvert, bridge, or grade dip so your road will not disrupt the natural flow of water (see Culverts, next page). Roads should crown slightly in the center so water runs off on either side.

Maintenance

By investing time in planning the position of your roadway and building a solid base, you'll minimize annual maintenance. Still, gravel roadways will always require some upkeep, including grading and patching ruts. Traffic will naturally press tracks into the surface, creating a larger crown down the center than desirable. You'll need to level this off and smooth out deep tracks to prevent drainage problems. This may call for filling uneven areas with more gravel and smoothing out the surface with a roller attachment.

The best preventive maintenance tool is your senses. Keep an eye on the land, watch for changes in topography, such as erosion. Anticipate roadblocks before you allow a rut to evolve into a pond. Small maintenance projects are far less consuming of time and resources than rebuilding a neglected byway.

WATER COURSES are carved in the ditch area next to a road to provide a benign route for water runoff.

Culverts

If your property contains streams or ditches that swell into creeks after a heavy rain, a culvert will allow you to safely cross these water flows. Rushing water can speed erosion, flood driveways, and disrupt the stability of land, spurring further drainage issues. A culvert works like a feeding tube, directing runoff water under roadways or along streambeds to prevent flooding.

Directing Drainage

Runoff and erosion are typical problems you'll face on the land. Instead of relying on a carefully mapped-out subdivision drainage plan executed by a developer, you'll need to implement your own drainage solutions. By now, you've gotten to know the lay of your land, and you can identify low-lying areas that are persistently wet and ditches that tend to overflow and flood.

A culvert that is used to manage runoff is often referred to as a cross drain. The goal is to transplant upland runoff that accumulates in ditches. Strategically placed culverts will move water and prevent flooding. Contact your county extension agent for advice on how to position a culvert. It must be installed at the proper grade, or sediment and debris will reduce its carrying capacity.

Crossing Streams

Even if the creeks and small streams on your property are dry most of the year, their steep beds present a land obstacle if you need to cross them with equipment—or even just by foot. To solve the problem, create an earth bridge supported by a culvert, which will double as the infrastructure for your bridge and a passageway for waters that rise during wet seasons. Water can pass through without damaging the earthen roadway. Also, a culvert will slow water speed to prevent flooding and resulting erosion. Always check with local regulations first before placing culverts and diverting waters.

IF A STREAM is prone to flooding, a culvert will protect the earthen bridge and help direct water toward a drainage area.

Buying Culverts

Culverts are corrugated tubes made from metal or plastic. Their rippled texture slows water velocity and provides a greater strength-to-weight ratio than smooth pipe. Culverts can support the weight of heavy equipment or vehicles. You can purchase culverts at farm or building supply stores. Or, you can check with a highway department, forest service, or bureau of land management to see whether they can sell you an old culvert in usable condition.

This is a general guide for installing a culvert in a streambed. Consult with a contractor or a county extension agent for further assistance.

1. Excavate the streambed 6" (15.2 cm). As you clear away soil, be sure to follow the slope, typically 2 to 6 percent. If the culvert is set too high, water will seep under the culvert and eventually wash out the road above it. Set too deep, a culvert will clog up with debris.

2. Spread a bed of soil or sand in the excavated area and compact it. The tamping will compress the 6" (15.2 cm) of fill down to 4" (10.2 cm). The 2" (5.1 cm) allowance will cradle the culvert.

3. Set the culvert in the streambed. Fill around it with layers of dirt and riprap at the inlet and outlet. Riprap is a loose assemblage of broken stones positioned to support the culvert and protect against erosion.

4. Plant grass or groundcover for added erosion protection.

Fences

Fencing plays a critical role in controlling animals, keeping out predators, sectioning off pastures, drawing property lines, and adding aesthetic appeal to properties. Your fencing needs will vary depending on the size of your lot and what type of animals call your land home (pigs, chickens, horses). Hobby farms will require functional fences, but if you live on a country estate, the reasons for your fence may be purely aesthetic. There are materials and designs that accommodate both goals.

Fence Materials

Progress in fencing is evident in the type of materials available, synthetics like PVC, and the improved life expectancy of good old standards like wood and wire, which can be treated with a vinyl coating. High-tensile wire fencing can last up to 50 years. But the more traditional types such as split-rail, Virginia rail, and post-and-rail will always have their place.

Before choosing fencing material, ask yourself the following: How large is the area to be fenced? What is the purpose of your fence? Will you install it yourself or hire a professional? How much are you willing to spend?

VINYL FENCING is durable and virtually maintenance free. However, damaged pieces are expensive to replace and materials can cost up to twice as much as a traditional wood fence. For these reasons, most landowners use vinyl to enclose smaller areas.

IN OLDEN DAYS, split-rail fences were hewn from logs taken out during the land clearing process. This can still be done, but more often they are made from purchased presplit rails and mortised posts.

Farm Fence Types

Wood: The split-rail fence (also called post-and-rail) that comes to mind when you think "country" isn't the best option for containing curious sheep or determined pigs, unless it is fortified with a layer of woven wire. But wood fences appeal to homeowners. They can be painted, stained, or left natural if made from cedar, cypress, black locust, or redwood, which contain natural preservatives. Choose wood if you're fencing in a small pasture, dividing a pasture (cross fencing), enclosing a riding area for horses, or for aesthetic appeal as a property boundary or divider between yard and the land you don't plan to mow so carefully.

Barbed wire: Although this type of fencing is not permitted in many cities and suburbs, it is the only feasible option for country lots in some states. Check with your county extension agent to find out if there are any restrictions in your area. Barbed wire isn't kind to the touch, so you may want to hire a professional to install it. For this reason, barbed wire isn't necessarily the best option if you want to contain animals without injuring them. A persistent pet that gets caught in the wire will be punished by its barbed points and rough surface.

Coated wire: This fencing is made from 12- to 14-gauge steel wire encased in high-tensile polymer or vinyl. The synthetic coating prevents rusting. Use coated-wire fencing as an alternative to traditional woven wire or barbed wire. You'll pay a bit more for coated fencing.

THIS MESH FENCE will prevent roaming sheep from escaping the pasture. Woven wire is popular for retaining animals, and a split-rail fence makes a simple boundary line.

If your property contains electric fences, be sure to install warning signs so neighbors and visitors understand that the barrier is wired, charged, and ready to zap.

Design

As you consider available materials, begin to plot out where you will place fences. Using graph paper, draw a sketch of your property and various elements that require boundaries. Label pastures, gardens, dog runs, and areas where you keep animals. You may decide to run a post-and-beam fence along your property line. Many veteran farmers will tell you that in the country, a fence, not a land survey, draws the line between properties. Still, consult the survey to determine how many square footage of fencing you will need.

More Fence Types

High-tensile wire: High-tensile wire can withstand significant wear and tear, and it is available in smooth and woven configurations. Hire a professional to install it. The material costs more than traditional options, but it will last a half century. Use a high-tensile wire fence to contain animals and to keep out predators.

Woven wire: Supported by wooden posts, woven wire is ideal for fencing in pigs, goats, sheep, chickens, or any animal known to burrow beneath or climb over synthetic barriers. (Pigs are especially guilty of rooting under and forcing through fences.) These fences also function well for horses.

PVC: This material represents the new school of fencing. Synthetic fencing stands up to the elements, so you won't worry about staining or replacing rusted-out woven wire. PVC fencing is available in many styles, mimicking a white picket fence, split-rail fence, or a fence with vertical rails (more suitable for aesthetic applications). You're more likely to see PVC fences in exurban areas or on farms that raise animals like alpacas.

High-tensile polymer: This barrier is made from tightly strung polymer strands.

Electric: The key to an effective electric fence is the quality of the fence charger, also called an energizer. This device sends out short pulses of energy—and you want those pulses to be short. Long, intense bursts of energy can harm animals rather than merely startle them. Look for a low-impedance unit, and do not shop based on price.

YOU WON'T WORRY about neighbors bringing your horses back home if you invest in a high-tensile wire fence.

VINYL FENCES withstand the elements and require little maintenance. They come in a wide array of styles but are usually white. Composite fences are made in a range of darker colors. Both types are relatively expensive.

VINYL FENCES consist of plastic rails and fence panels that fit into slots in plastic posts cladding. (The cladding either fits over a 4 x 4 post or is filled with concrete after installation.)

COMPOSITE FENCING SYSTEMS are relatively expensive but are quite durable and are available in a wider range of colors and textures than PVC fences. Their assembly process is similar.

Vinyl and composite fences require little maintenance and can last a lifetime (if they don't get hit by a truck or caught in a brushfire). This low-maintenance longevity justifies the high initial cost for many. Manufacturers of both vinyl and composite fences claim that they are less expensive than wood in the long run, when you factor in the repair, refinishing, and eventual replacement of wood fences as the years pass.

Vinyl fences are made from polyvinyl chloride (PVC), the same plastic used in vinyl house siding and waste pipes. Vinyl fencing is co-extruded with an outside layer that includes titanium dioxide. This is the same compound found in sunscreen, and it protects the plastic from degradation by ultraviolet (UV) sun rays. Because titanium dioxide is white, vinyl fencing is most commonly available in bright white, although PVC products with light tan and gray coloring are starting to hit the market.

Composite fences are made from a blend of wood fibers and plastic resins (some resins are recycled from grocery bags). The wood fiber provides strength and UV protection while the plastic keeps the material from absorbing water and rotting. In the world of synthetic fences, composite fence manufacturers claim the en-

vironmental high ground. The manufacturing of composite lumber has not been linked to dioxin pollution, as PVC production has been. Composites can also be produced in darker colors than PVC and with an assortment of surface textures.

Vinyl fencing has been around longer than composite fencing, and it comes in almost as many styles as wood fencing. Traditionally, after constructing a vinyl fence, rebar rods were put into some or all of the hollow posts, and then the posts were filled partway with concrete. This is still the way most pros build vinyl fences. DIY-friendly vinyl and composite fences are available with posts that are essentially hollow sleeves designed to fit over standard pressure-treated 4 × 4 posts.

Vinyl and composite fencing is assembled from pre-manufactured components and panels. This makes it difficult to adjust the length of fence sections should your post spacing be off. (You can cut the rails, but you can't increase their length.) For this reason, you need to either set the posts as you go or be very meticulous with your all-at-the-same-time post spacing and leveling. If the terrain is uneven or the soil is full of roots or rocks, consider setting one post at a time.

THE VIRGINIA RAIL FENCE exhibits a very familiar style to anyone who has spent much time in countryside that was cleared and farmed in the 18th and 19th centuries. Since nails were scarce, these zigzagging post-and-rail fences were popular because they are held together with only wire or rope.

Virginia Rail Fence

The Virginia rail fence—also called a worm, snake, or zigzag fence—was actually considered the national fence by the U.S. Department of Agriculture prior to the advent of wire fences in the late 1800s. All states with farmland cleared from forests had them in abundance. The simplest fences were built with an extreme zigzag and didn't require posts. To save on lumber and land, farmers began straightening the fences and burying pairs of posts at the rail junctures.

A variation in design that emerged with entirely straight lines is called a Kentucky rail fence.

Feel free to accommodate the overlapping rail fence we build here to suit your tastes and needs. Increase the zigzag to climb rolling ground, decrease it to stretch the fence out. All lapped rail fences should be made from rot-resistant wood like cedar, locust, or cyprus. For the most authentic-looking fence, try to find split rather than sawn logs. For longevity, raise the bottom rail off the ground with stones. Posts may eventually rot below ground, but the inherently stable zigzag form should keep the fence standing until you can replace them.

Build a Virginia Rail Fence

Lay out three or four sections of fence rails without posts along your fence line to get a sense of how much overlap, zigzag, and height you want. Vary the side-to-side offset of the rail junctures. More extreme zigzags accommodate rolling land better and are more stable, but they require more space and lumber. Vary the height of your prototype. Be aware that your finished fence will ride higher when the rails are set on top of rocks or wired between posts and shimmed.

PROJECT

TOOLS & MATERIALS

- Tools & materials for laying out the fence line
- Tools & materials for setting posts
- Chainsaw or reciprocating saw
- Long-handled maul
- Large screwdriver
- Bolt cutters
- Pliers
- Hatchet
- Clothesline rope

How to Build a Virginia Rail Fence

1. Create layout lines in the fence installation area for each section. Mark post locations and a main fence line with additional layout lines parallel to the fence line. The total distance between the outer lines (here, 24") equals the amount of switchback on each rail section. Dig your post holes and install your posts.

2. Bind your post pairs together at the top and place spacers on the ground for the bottom rail. Insert the bottom rail between the posts, resting on the spacers.

3. Install split fence rails in alternating courses at each post pair, keeping the overhangs even.

4. Bind the tops of the posts together permanently with 9-gauge galvanized wire to hold the rails in position. Tighten the wire by twisting with a screwdriver blade as if you were tightening a tourniquet.

Windbreaks

Wind is a constant combatant for landowners. It saps heat from homes, whips up nearly insurmountable snowdrifts, and stings animals with its frigid blast. In summer, it slaps against crops, stirs up soil and dust, and can damage farm structures in especially severe conditions. Regardless of the size of your land, you can protect your best interests—your home, shed, barn, animals, and pocketbook—with effective windbreaks.

Windbreaks are plantings or screens that slow, direct, and block wind from protected areas. Reduction in wind speed can help conserve energy and control snow. If executed properly, your windbreak will enhance the landscape and function as a shelterbelt.

The Anatomy of a Windbreak

This discussion pertains to natural windbreaks comprised of shrubs, conifers, and deciduous trees. You can certainly purchase screening or secure fences with heavy boards or canvas to block wind. But an aesthetically pleasing, long-term solution requires installing strategic rows of plant material.

The components of an effective windbreak include height, width, density, and orientation. Height and width come with age, and your windbreak may require 20 years to mature. This is where density comes in. Even young trees can block wind if they are placed in rows. Density depends on the number of rows, type of foliage, and gaps. No windbreak is 100 percent dense, but those with 60 to 80 percent density will protect a small yard area or a modest farmstead. The larger the area being protected, the less foliage density is required for protection. To prevent snowdrifts, only a 25 to 35 percent density is necessary.

Orientation involves placing rows of plants at right angles to the wind for best results. Keep in mind, wind direction may change with the seasons, so determine whether a multiple-leg windbreak is necessary. Concerning length, a rule of thumb is to plant a windbreak that is ten times longer than its greatest height.

A WINDBREAK OF MATURE EVERGREENS will protect a structure from damaging gusts, potentially reducing energy bills.

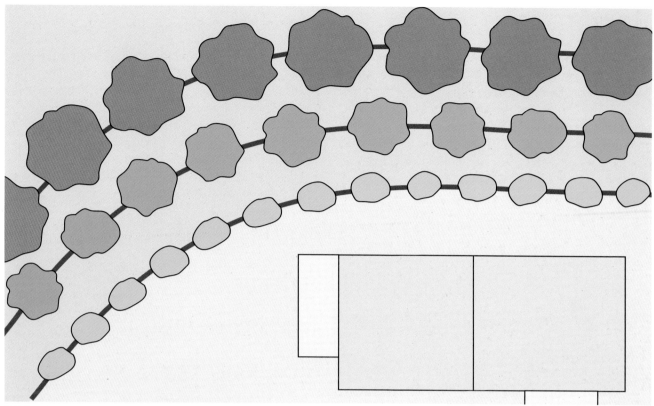

THREE ROWS of staggered trees serve as a protective block.

Plant Material and Design

To achieve the density required to block wind, plant at least a few rows of trees. Plant short trees or shrubs upwind and taller trees downwind. If your windbreak borders your home, choose attractive plants for the inside row. Buffer this with rows of evergreens and dense species that will break the wind year-round.

Density plays a significant role in windbreak design. Ideally, plant at least three rows of trees. The inside row of a narrow windbreak should be at least 75 feet (22.9 m) from buildings or structures, with the outside row 100 to 150 feet (30.5 to 45.7 m) away. Within this 25- to 75-foot (7.6 to 22.9 m) area, plant rows 16 to 20 feet (4.9 to 6.1 m) apart for shrubs and conifers and no closer than 14 feet (4.3 m) for deciduous trees. Within rows, space trees so their foliage can mature and eventually improve the density. Narrow spacing is a short-term solution because cramped trees don't fill out to their full capacity.

A windbreak improves as you add more tree rows. But this is not always possible, especially near the home. While single-row windbreaks are not nearly as effective, they suffice when plants are evergreen trees planted with as few gaps as possible. A twin-row windbreak will also work in limited space. Again, opt for evergreens or shrubs planted close together. Stagger trees so that a gap in the first row is protected by a tree in the second row.

You can plant curved rows of plants, which are appealing in a landscape setting. Just be sure to consult with a landscape designer or a university extension agent who can advise on ways to accomplish this without compromising the integrity of the windbreak.

Windbreak Benefits

Windbreaks deliver multiple benefits to your property.

Energy conservation: reduce energy costs from 20 to 40 percent

Snow control: single rows of shrubs function as snow fences

Privacy: block a roadside view and protect animals from exposure to passers-by

Noise control: muffle the sound of traffic if your pastures or home is near a road

Aesthetic appeal: improve your landscape and increase the value of your property

Erosion control: prevent dust from blowing; roots work against erosion

Barns

The barn is an icon of Americana and rural living—a stately fixture and the soul of a rural property. Even when weathered with missing boards and chipped paint, a barn exudes rustic charm. For this reason, some people decide to build a barn structure for their homes, while hobby farmers may remodel existing barns to include creature comforts—from Internet access to cozy offices.

The barn is a home base for storing equipment, as well as an ideal space to tinker with projects. If you plan to raise animals, you may prioritize barn improvements over redecorating your home. Perhaps the barn is serving as a supersized storage locker now, but you have grand plans to convert it into a hobby shop or home office. Maybe you're starting from scratch. Regardless, there are certain features you must include for functional purposes and plenty of bells and whistles that make today's barns a home away from home.

THE CLASSIC RED BARN instantly places us on the farm.

A BARN CAN BE USED to store just about anything, but if your barn houses animals then plan storage space for supplies such as hay.

Construction and Comfort

Before building or remodeling a barn, know your site, needs, and budget. If you are starting from the ground up, investigate some of the prefabricated barns on the market. Many times, the manufacturers will send a professional to manage the project. Otherwise, you can consult with an architect or site planner to design a barn that will suit your needs. Go to the table with clear goals for how you will use the space. A barn built for horses requires specific stall sizes that aren't mandatory for goats, for example. If equipment storage is the goal, the barn layout will not include stalls at all.

Following are some barn basics and extra features you may consider as you begin designing your new barn or remodeling an existing one.

The Basics

Site selection is critical if you want a dry, well-ventilated barn that's cool in the summer and toasty in the winter. You want to easily access your barn from your driveway or a thruway, and be sure you don't build it on a lowland, where water will run off and cause flooding. Think about wind patterns. If you live in the southwest, you may want to position your barn so wind can blow through doors on both ends like a breezeway. But in other regions, you'll fight to warm the barn if winter wind can blow right through the structure. Consider these variables.

Your foundation should consist of concrete aisles and a compacted surface in animal stalls. Crushed limestone screening tamps into a sturdy surface and is porous enough to drain well. Straw or wood chips are typical stall liners, and you can always add rubber mats to give animals' legs a bit of shock absorption. If your barn will house equipment and a workshop, you may opt to pour concrete floors throughout.

Solar power is a wise option for barns, even if installation costs are higher than traditional materials. You won't have to run power lines, you'll save on energy bills, and you can heat the barn and water with the system. If your barn has the capability of generating more power than it needs, you can even connect to the grid and run the power meter backward. Another energy saver is a tankless hot water heater, which heats water on demand rather than wasting energy to heat and store hot water. Check into federal tax credits if you decide to build or renovate a barn with these or other energy efficient options.

A functional barn includes plenty of electrical outlets, and you'll probably want to install a bathroom. You don't necessarily need a sewer hookup to do this. Consider a composting or incinerating toilet. Composting toilets don't flush, so they will not require water or a sewage system. Incinerating toilets use electricity.

Don't forget to equip your barn with fire extinguishers.

CUSTOMIZE THE FLOOR PLAN of your barn to accommodate animals and equipment.

The Extras

If you can dream it, you can design it into your barn. Beyond a bathroom, you may install a kitchenette with a small refrigerator. You won't have to worry about neglecting animals while you work from home if you build an office into your barn. While you're at it, carve room for a lounge area with a big-screen television. While this sounds extravagant, if you're in the horse business and you want to show a potential customer your Best in Show, you can conveniently cue up a video without leaving the barn. You may even install surveillance equipment so you can have a big-screen view of other areas of your land.

Loft spaces can double as storage and mini-apartments. You may design parlors for milking, tack rooms for dressing horses, and storage areas with cabinetry. If you show your animals, why not build in a trophy display? Some hobby farmers start modest side businesses by selling farm goods, so the barn is a convenient setting for a "storefront."

Equipment and Storage

If the sole purpose of your barn is to store equipment— and over time you'll accumulate plenty of it—focus on accessibility and allow room to expand your fleet. If your long-term plan includes upgrading your tractor and purchasing several new attachments, build a barn that will accommodate these new work toys.

A common mistake is to build barn doors that aren't wide or tall enough for equipment to pass through the opening. Clearance is the key here. Also, allow space inside the barn so you can maneuver power equipment. Wall storage units will help you organize your tools, and a workspace provides room to tinker with equipment or pursue carpentry projects. Allow extra room for storing "stuff." (You can never have too much storage.)

Animal Accoutrements

Housing animals requires a whole different approach to barn design than using the structure simply as an over-sized outbuilding for storage. Animals need fresh air and clean ground, fresh water and room to move around. Not all animals require stalls, but horses and cows do. If you raise alpacas, you'll separate the females and males, while goats, chickens, and pigs live communally. Allow room for hay storage and a separate space for cleaning or milking.

Here is a checklist of features to consider for various animals:

- Standard box stall for horses is 12 × 12 feet (3.7 × 3.7 m); stallion and brood mare stalls are usually 12 × 24 feet (3.7 by 7.3 meters)
- Chickens require 2 to 3 sq. feet (0.6 to .9 sq. m) per bird; 16 to 25 chickens fit in a 6 × 8 foot (1.8 × 2.4 m) enclosure.

- Cows can weigh up to 1,000 lb. (450 kg), so don't skimp on the stall construction.
- Stalls can be made of wood, steel, or wood with steel frames.
- Walls dividing stalls may be solid or partially open with grills or bars at the top.
- Open-grid stall doors allow for adequate ventilation.
- A compacted floor is best for animals; add rubber mats for additional cushioning.
- Ideally, a sliding barn door will open into a fenced run or pasture.
- Wash bays with French drains won't clog; an overhead, rotating hose mount eases the job of cleaning animals.
- Skylights, windows, and wide doors allow for plenty of sunlight and fresh air.
- A video surveillance system will allow you to watch animals from your computer at home.

A HORSE leans out of the open window of its stall, which allows enough room for it to move around comfortably.

Outbuildings

Improving the land often leads to equipment purchases and more tools and gadgets. Where will you store all of this stuff? Outbuildings provide extra covered space to protect all of the capital investments you make as you build your arsenal of "toys." If your property is a large estate, a sizable shed is a logical alternative to a barn. But even those with barns find that storage space is at a premium. An outbuilding just may provide the extra room required.

Outbuildings can function as workshops, greenhouses, and equipment storage facilities. They're versatile and easy to acquire with the selection of prefabricated options on the market. Before building any structure on your property, contact the county building department for zoning regulations and permit requirements.

Shed Kits

If you're handy, you can follow a shed plan or build one from scratch. But with all of the other improvements you're probably making to your land, why not save yourself the labor and investigate the array of shed kits and pole barns.

If you decide to purchase a kit, check the thickness of the lumber. Be sure it is treated. Is the flooring high quality, and what is the overlap structure of the panels? Thick flooring will bear the weight of heavy equipment, and snug panels prevent water leakage. Consider the size of the shed and what features are important to you.

OUTBUILDINGS such as storage sheds, chicken coops, and greenhouses provide extra storage on a hobby farm.

Mini-barn

A SPACIOUS SHED can be designed to match the color and style of a nearby barn, as with the gambrel-style shed seen here.

A CONCRETE SLAB FOUNDATION and all-wood construction are important if you want your shed to last.

INEXPENSIVE SIDING PANELS such as T1-11 paneling are durable and easy to install.

A LARGE GARAGE DOOR is important if your shed will house farm vehicles.

What's the Function?

For gardeners, a shed provides a convenient shelter for storing pots and can be equipped with a workspace for planting and related activities. You'll want skylights or windows so the shed gets light exposure and fresh air. If you simply want to clear out a garage that is overrun with equipment, you may prefer a shed without windows. That way, contents are secure and not visible.

Storage Capacity

How much space do you really need? Deconstructed shed kits are deceiving, so you should not eyeball a kit and assume that it will fit your needs. If you jam equipment and tools in a shed, you'll end up unloading half of its contents every time you need to reach something wedged in the back. Your outbuilding should be large enough so that you can walk in, find what you need, and easily access it. That also means allowing space to drive tractors and lawn equipment in and out of the opening.

One way to estimate space requirements is to lay out on the lawn all of the contents you will store in your shed. Space equipment so you can maneuver it with ease, and group tools you will hang on the walls. Mainly, you want to assess the surface area you'll need, so focus on laying out items that will sit on the shed's foundation. Stake the area and attach strings to stakes to form a square or rectangle. Measure this space, and choose your shed kit accordingly.

Metal Shed Kit

IF YOU NEED AN OUTBUILDING now and don't have the time or inclination to build one from scratch, a shed kit is the answer. Better kits are made with quality long-lasting parts, and some come largely preassembled for ease of installation.

METAL KIT SHEDS aren't glamorous, but if you're looking for utility, low cost, and quick assembly, a shed kit with a steel frame and enameled steel panels is tough to beat.

A METAL KIT BASE that's anchored to a patch of compacted gravel provides good drainage.

ASSEMBLING KIT SHEDS can take some patience, but with a couple of power tools the job will go quickly.

Hoophouse

SOME OUTBUILDINGS are more permanent than others. The hoophouse is used mostly as a temporary shelter for seedlings or for the shelter and comfort of the gardener who's potting out in the field. The materials for a hoophouse are cheap, and making your own is easy.

A HOOPHOUSE is a temporary agricultural structure made from PVC tubes and plastic.

THE PVC PIPES that make the frame are friction-fit together so they require no glue.

THE PLASTIC SHEETING used for the cover is attached only at the ends, but it must be weighted down all the way along the base.

CHAPTER 3

Maintaining Your Land

You need an arsenal of equipment to care for your land, though the necessities depend on acreage, land use, and how much of the work you do yourself. A large property requires bigger machines with more horsepower—equipment that can dig, haul, and do just about any job with the change of an attachment. A big backyard may call for an efficient mower and hand-held power equipment. Regardless of your land care needs, the right equipment and tools enable you to accomplish regular maintenance and special projects with less manpower and energy.

A LAWN TRACTOR WITH ATTACHMENTS, such as this cart, can take a load off hauling and lifting projects.

Equipment Essentials

Whether your property is three acres or fifty acres, you'll quickly learn that the equipment stored in your garage won't cut it when it comes to country-size maintenance. A trusty push mower is just fine for maneuvering into hard-to-reach areas on a city lot, but even a self-propelled engine isn't enough to relieve the labor burden on a large estate. A handcart is fine for hauling topsoil to a backyard garden, but you'll need horsepower and a loader to dig, scrape, and move materials on a hobby farm.

The first order of business when acquiring equipment is to refer back to your land plan. Will your projects require heavy-duty hauling, lifting, grappling, and rough-cutting? Or, is your main goal to mow lots of grass fast?

The land plan plays an important role in your buying decision because you must consider your needs beyond today. This week you are mowing five acres. But next year, you plan to clear an area overtaken with multiflora. And the year after that, you expect to raise a barn. During this point, you'll build a fence. So you see, your equipment needs expand beyond mowing. Equipment dealers will advise you to buy up. Don't invest handsomely in a lawn tractor if you know you'll need a skid steer loader next year. The biggest mistakes new landowners make are 1) underestimating horsepower needs; 2) failing to consider equipment size limitations; and 3) buying too much equipment too fast. You can avoid all of this by explaining your land plan to a reputable equipment dealer.

Before you visit a dealer, check out manufacturers' websites to educate yourself about helpful tools in all the major equipment categories: lawn and garden, compact tractors, and utility tractors. You can find out what price range to expect and what type of equipment will accomplish your maintenance needs.

Your Equipment Dealer

When you move to a new area, it's comforting to have a resource who can answer questions and offer that "been there, done that" perspective on land, equipment, mechanics, and where to find the best hay, feed, and advice.

Your local equipment dealer can guide you toward machines that make sense for your land. As you determine what type of mower, tractor, and handheld equipment you need to manage your property, a dealer will educate you on important subjects like power, torque, and weight.

BEFORE YOU PURCHASE A TRACTOR OR UTILITY VEHICLE, measure the height of the doorway of your storage area. Be sure the roll-over-protection-system (ROPS) bar will fit through the opening or avoid clearance issues by purchasing a folding ROPS.

Mowing Equipment

There's the yard—the manicured carpet of green surrounding your home—and the pasture, and the wild, grassy area beyond. These spots call for different mowing equipment and techniques. Your property may contain one or both scenarios, in which case versatility becomes a key factor in your equipment purchase. Big backyards call for lawn tractors or zero-turn mowers that can efficiently accomplish a cut. You'll need a compact utility tractor for properties that also require rough-cutting (bush-hogging) to knock down knee-high grasses. Base your buying decision on these factors:

- **Will you only mow grass?**
- **Does the grass require a finished cut?**
- **Do you plan to take on additional projects, such as clearing land or building a fence?**
- **What maintenance will you do yourself, and what tasks will you delegate to professionals?**

Just Grass

Big backyards benefit from efficient zero-turn-radius (ZTR) mowers, which were first introduced in the commercial market. You've probably seen landscape contractors zip around properties on these front-cut mowers. Now, there are models designed for consumers

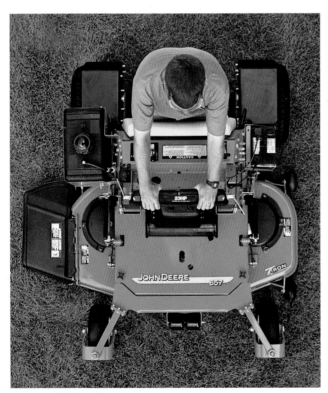

MORE HOMEOWNERS are choosing commercial-grade zero-turn-radius (ZTR) mowers because of their efficiency and the quality, finish cut they provide.

that range from 19 to 30 horsepower, though you can purchase commercial equipment for your land even if you aren't the owner of a landscape company.

ZTRs deliver a finished cut—golf-course quality, in some cases—and will save you time mowing turf that matters. This machine will suit your needs if your entire estate is grass and you plan to hire a pro to build retaining walls and dig fences. ZTRs turn on a dime, swiveling 180 degrees or more with ease. The fast-moving mowers are fun to operate once you get the hang of the twin-lever steering controls. The only downside to ZTRs is they accept limited attachments beyond a bagger. They are also more difficult to handle on slopes than lawn tractors.

Of course, there are riding mowers that only cut grass (as opposed to lawn and garden tractors that accept attachments and can multitask) and the traditional push mower that manages hard-to-reach areas. If you choose one of these two options, you'll likely end up buying additional equipment to manage jobs such as hauling bags of feed or pushing snow. A riding mower is not quite as efficient as a ZTR for cutting grass, and it only cuts turf.

Lawn and Garden Tractors

A lawn and garden tractor will mow and work on other small-scale projects. The key words are "lawn and garden." The tractor's capabilities are limited to landscape tasks. As a lighter-duty riding mower, attachments allow the machine to also lift materials, till gardens, and push snow. They are versatile, and some models provide rugged, all-terrain capabilities. Lawn and garden tractors generally range from 19 to 25 horsepower with cutting decks up to 62 inches (15.7 cm) at the high end. But as with all equipment, lawn tractors have limitations. They offer peak performance for big backyards but they aren't quite tough enough for hobby farms. When land clearing, heavy hauling, and deep digging are involved, upgrade to a utility tractor. Most landowners who own several acres will bypass the lawn and garden tractor option and "buy up." They may opt for a ZTR or riding mower for the lawn area surrounding their house, then rely on a utility tractor for other labor.

Tractors

A tractor is the hardest-working piece of farm equipment you'll buy. Depending on which class it belongs to, a tractor will bale hay, mow large fields, dig trenches, grade land, grapple and transport small trees, and move loads you couldn't possibly manage by hand. As you cultivate the land and build your dream hobby farm or

Anatomy of a Mower

Get to know the components of your equipment so you will understand its capabilities and limitations.

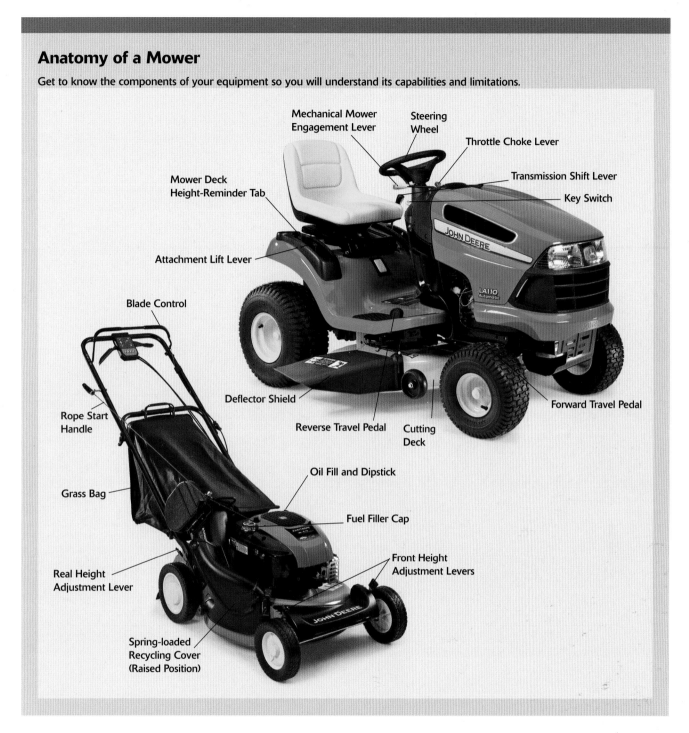

- Mechanical Mower Engagement Lever
- Steering Wheel
- Throttle Choke Lever
- Transmission Shift Lever
- Key Switch
- Mower Deck Height-Reminder Tab
- Attachment Lift Lever
- Blade Control
- Rope Start Handle
- Grass Bag
- Deflector Shield
- Reverse Travel Pedal
- Cutting Deck
- Forward Travel Pedal
- Oil Fill and Dipstick
- Fuel Filler Cap
- Real Height Adjustment Lever
- Front Height Adjustment Levers
- Spring-loaded Recycling Cover (Raised Position)

great estate, you'll spend quality time with your tractor. So choose one you can keep for years. When you talk tractors with your dealer, he or she will classify machines based on horsepower, torque, and weight. Here's what you need to know:

Horsepower: Gross horsepower is the amount of power the engine produces. This power must also carry the weight of the tractor. PTO is power takeoff—the oomph factor. PTO is gross horsepower minus the power consumed by the machine. That's what's leftover to power attachments and manage loads. When shopping, compare PTO power among tractors.

Torque: This is the working capacity of the tractor, the rotational force that can move loads.

Weight: Tractor weight is equated with working power. Once you add an attachment to a machine, you consume working power. Certain attachments, such as hay balers, require heavier machines and more power. Consider what jobs you want to accomplish and how much stress that will put on your machine.

If you will use a piece of equipment or an attachment only for a day's time, consider renting it or bartering with a neighbor who owns what you need. Before you invest in a tractor, ask the dealer about testing it, or consider renting one of a similar model.

UTILITY TRACTORS can manage heavy-duty jobs such as moving trees and clearing and making hay.

Compact Tractors

A compact tractor should have enough power and versatility to support the maintenance of properties up to most landowners with less than 150 acres; and 30 to 40 horsepower is enough to rough-cut pastures, till fields, manage a good working load, and do all the lifting, digging, and moving that most hobby farms require. A compact tractor is a less wieldy cousin of the industrial utility tractor that is most often used in commercial agricultural applications. The real work force of a tractor is its implements (see Compact Tractor Attachments on pages 66 and 67).

Utility Tractors

This is the granddaddy of tractors, designed for big farms with lots of land and a wide range of chores that need doing. Horsepower ranges from 45 to 110. You can invest in a utility tractor that is suitable for 10 to 20 acres and can manage a hay baler. This may be appropriate if you want a tractor that will get most jobs done. The difference between compact and utility tractors is power, weight, and work capacity. If you are considering a high-end compact tractor, consider buying up to a midrange utility tractor.

UTILITY VEHICLES ARE EXCELLENT BACK SAVERS when used instead of labor-intensive wheelbarrows or handcarts.

Utility Vehicles

Utility vehicles are rugged machines designed to transport loads. You'll traverse your land faster and more conveniently on four wheels. Some utility vehicles are strictly for hauling and moving, while others have the versatility of a tractor. All-terrain vehicles can effortlessly cross rough land and drive through streams and mud holes. You can purchase trailers and attachments that transform utility vehicles into real workhorses. Meanwhile, some lighter-duty models are just right for property owners who want a quick way to zip from one place to the next without lugging tools and gardening essentials with a handcart.

Compact Tractor Attachments

Without attachments that are designed to get specific jobs done, a tractor is little more than a way to get from point A to point B. With a full menu of helpful attachments, you can accomplish tasks from mowing to grading.

Mowing: A mid-mount (belly mount) mower attachment produces a finish cut for manicured areas. Rear-mount rotary attachments allow you to rough-cut large land tracts.

Loading: The loader is a multipurpose essential for digging, scraping, light grading, and moving. Once you have a loader, you can add these tools to accomplish specific tasks:

> **4-in-1 bucket:** load, scrape, blade, and clamp materials
>
> **Bale spears:** carry round hay bales
>
> **Grapple:** carry hard-to-handle items like tree limbs and stumps
>
> **Forks:** lift and move loads.

Snow removal: Brush snow surfaces with a rotary broom or attach a snow blower.

Digging: Backhoes break through tough, compacted soil.

Aerating: Core aerating tool reduces soil compaction.

Tilling: Strong tines till up garden beds and ground.

Spreading: Broadcast and pendular spreaders distribute seeds and granular fertilizer products.

A RIDING MOWER will accept attachments and function as much more than a grass-cutting machine. For this reason, some hobby farmers choose a lawn and garden tractor over a zero-turn radius mower.

BALING YOUR OWN HALE requires an investment in tools, which is why some land owners purchase hay or hire out the job of harvesting and baling the crop.

THIS SKID-STEER LOADER with a snow thrower attachment is ideal for gravel roads because it will not scrape up the rocks.

LARGER AGRICULTURAL CLASS EQUIPMENT like this tractor can pull attachments designed to level the land.

THIS BOX RAKE helps a land owner grade the surface, creating a level area that will prevent drainage issues by the barn.

Tools of the Trade

The right tools make quick work of any job. Before you buy out the farm and fleet store and take home every tool at the garden store, stop. Consider your hobbies: gardening, caring for animals, raising crops, basic landscaping. This staple of basic hand tools will accomplish most tasks on large estates and hobby farms.

Gardening

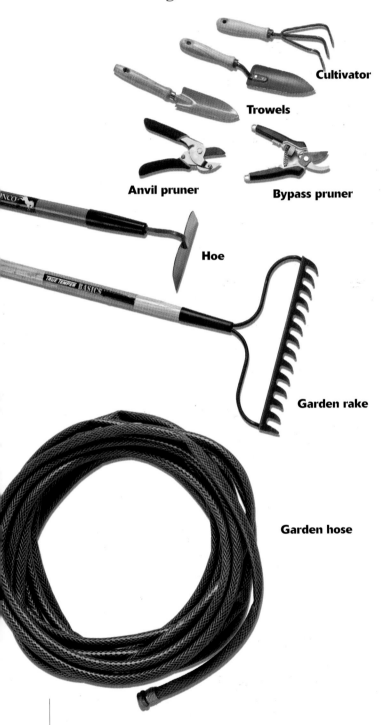

Cultivator

Trowels

Anvil pruner

Bypass pruner

Hoe

Garden rake

Garden hose

Lawn and Landscaping

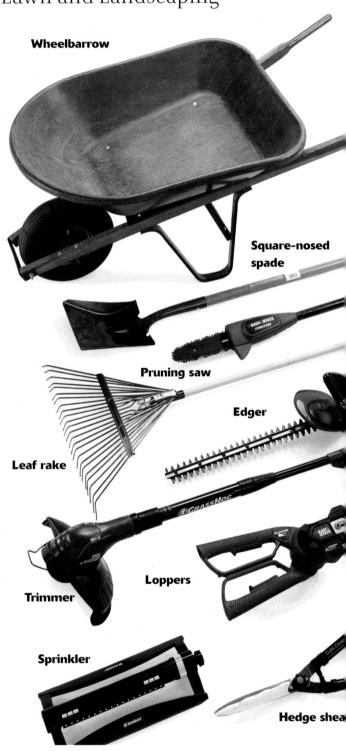

Wheelbarrow

Square-nosed spade

Pruning saw

Edger

Leaf rake

Loppers

Trimmer

Sprinkler

Hedge shea[rs]

Carpentry

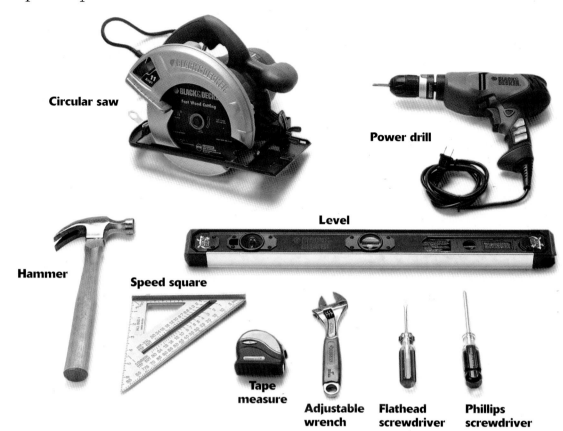

Circular saw

Power drill

Hammer

Level

Speed square

Tape measure

Adjustable wrench

Flathead screwdriver

Phillips screwdriver

Land Basics

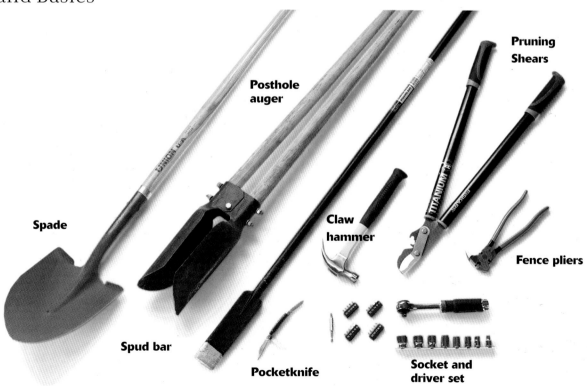

Posthole auger

Pruning Shears

Spade

Claw hammer

Fence pliers

Spud bar

Pocketknife

Socket and driver set

Avoid confusing lawn mower and two-cycle equipment fuels by keeping two separate gas containers in your garage or shed. Distinguish them with marker or colored tape, or purchase different colored containers.

EDGING MACHINES have a circular blade that digs and cuts into turf. Clean up the perimeter of your lawn by scooting an edger along the sidewalk or driveway to slice off unruly edges. A string trimmer will clean up edges (above) but it won't produce the clean line that a stick edger will. Eye protection is always recommended when operating handheld power equipment.

Handheld Power Equipment

You need two-cycle equipment like a string trimmer, stick edger, and blower to maintain your landscape. You can use a trimmer to clean up the lawn perimeter, but it will not produce the manicured look that an edger will.

POWER BLOWERS are available in handheld and backpack styles. They are convenient for collecting leaves and removing dirt and debris from patio and driveway areas.

STRING TRIMMERS use a whipping motion to cut grass and are designed for trimming around trees, along bed edges and lawn perimeters, and in areas that mowers cannot easily access.

Aerate or Dethatch?

Aeration literally airs out soil and unplugs cores of turf by mild agitation with an aerator machine or an aerator attachment that hitches to your tractor. Removing turf plugs restores air and water circulation to roots and makes room for new growth come spring.

Dethatching, also called verticutting, is a slicing action whereby rotating blades cut into the turf, pulling up dead and dry remains of turf roots and plants. If you notice strawlike turf remnants sitting underneath healthy sprigs of green grass, then thatch is the problem.

Aeration and dethatching are often confused. They are similar because both processes agitate the lawn and break up soil and turf to promote healthier growth. Both involve machines with tines, but dethatching is far more aggressive. Aeration can remedy light thatch coverage. Aerating is basically a no-brainer job. Rent an aerator, and operate it similarly to how you run a push lawn mower. Before aerating, check soil temperature and moisture level. Be sure the lawn is moist but not drenched. A little moisture will soften the ground and allow the core cutter to work efficiently; too much moisture and you will turn your lawn into a mud pie. Mark irrigation system heads, pet tie-ups, and other stakes or fixtures in the ground. Aeration is a fall project for cool-season grasses. Wear gloves because walk-behind aerators are tough on the hands. Be sure to clear the property of debris and other obstacles that may get in the way, such as a dog line or irrigation system spray heads. These can damage the equipment.

TURF PLUGS ARE A SOURCE OF NITROGEN and nutrients. Allow them to decompose so your soil can reap the benefits.

TREAT YOUR LAWN AREA by ensuring that roots receive the nutrients necessary to thrive. Aerating removes turf and soil plugs, and it gives your yard some breathing room so it can grow healthy.

Lawn Care Tools

You hold higher expectations for your lawn than the field beyond it. In many ways your yard is a welcome mat, showing visitors that you maintain and care for your property. Also, there's the curb appeal factor. A lush, green lawn is aesthetically pleasing, and treating this space special separates the "people zone" from areas where animals graze.

Safety

Always wear eye protection when operating string trimmers, edgers, or any handheld equipment. Hearing protection is suggested when operating equipment that produces noise of 85 decibels or more. Most gas-powered lawn mowers and string trimmers exceed this level.

LOOK FOR SEED THAT WILL PROVIDE LUSH, GREEN TURFGRASS in the designated lawn areas of your land. While wild prairie turf is suitable for areas beyond your formal yard, you may want to plan for more residential turf species near your home, barn, and other areas frequently tread upon.

Seeding

If you live on several acres, you may choose to establish a lawn area and dedicate the rest of the land to pasture. In that case, the type of seed you plant in these areas will differ greatly. Depending on your region, you will plant turfgrasses like Kentucky bluegrass, St. Augustine grass, fescue, and perennial ryegrass in your yard. Pasture and field grass will vary based on the animals that eat there. For instance, dairy cattle love alfalfa, but this plant makes horses sick if not "diluted" with other forage. Talk to a county extension agent for advice.

Planting a Lawn

Before you plant a new lawn, conduct a soil pH test to determine whether the ground contains the proper balance of nutrients—nitrogen, phosphorus, and potassium—that the turf requires (see Soil Study on page 84). Consider your turfgrass climate zone and choose a high-quality seed that will produce a thick, green lawn. You can hire a landscape contractor to seed your property; a professional has the broadcast spreader equipment necessary to do the job efficiently. Or, you can seed it yourself: till soil; spread seed; work seed into soil with a landscape rake; protect

with hay to prevent moisture loss; and water regularly. All this can be done on smaller lawn areas (½ acre) with the help of a lawn tractor with a tilling attachment and a walk-behind broadcast spreader.

The top mistake people make when seeding a lawn occurs during the spreading process. Seeds need breathing room to sprout, so you must calibrate your broadcast spreader so it distributes the recommended amount of seed. That is generally 5 to 10 pounds. (2.3 to 4.5 kg) per 1,000 square feet (92.9 sq. m). Also, for the first three weeks of a seed's life, you must keep the top ¼ inch (6 mm) of soil moist. Do this with sprinklers or an in-ground irrigation system.

Did You Know?

There are more than 75,000 species of grass, and they include plants such as corn, sorghum, and bamboo. Roughly 75 of these grasses can withstand repeated grazing, and half of those are grasses you'd want to grow in your lawn.

Plant a Pasture

The grass you grow in your pasture can provide valuable nutrition for farm animals, including cows, sheep, and horses. What's more, grass will reduce erosion and decrease weed pressure. Your animals will stay healthier because grass helps control parasites and dust. But not just any grass will do. The general rule of thumb is to plant 40 percent legumes, including clover and alfalfa. Your goal is to establish a healthy mix of plants to feed animals.

Just because a pasture looks untamed does not mean you're relieved of weed control duties. Remember, your land is a giant salad bowl for pet animals. Strain out the bad stuff so they don't get sick by removing poisonous plants and undesirable weeds from your pasture. Also, take care when using chemical weed sprays. Most veterinarians do not recommend them.

A BROADCAST SPREADER attachment on a compact utility tractor is used to spread grass seed efficiently over large acreage.

FOR OPTIMAL HEALTH, the usual seed mixture for horse pastures is part grass and part legume. Horses can become fatally ill if they consume certain types of grasses or weeds, so be sure to discuss appropriate pasture types with your local state extension office, feed mill, and vet. Also be sure to have a professional analysis done on existing pastures before moving horses into the area.

ALL COWS NEED AT LEAST SOME FORAGE (grass, legumes, or silage) to remain healthy. They are often fed additional grain, soy, and other ingredients to maintain nutrition. Cows raised on a diet primarily composed of pasture are now classified as grass fed. Many consumers now prefer the taste and nutritional benefits of grass-fed beef.

Planting Trees

Trees provide many benefits to any property. Windbreaks are often necessary landscape infrastructure, and these live barriers require planting trees that guard protected areas from the elements (see page 48). Or, your property's landscape could be a blank canvas; installing shrubs and yearling trees will add interest to your land. Whether you plant trees for functional or purely aesthetic purposes, this project will guide you through the steps of how to plant a tree.

Before You Plant

The best time to plant trees is spring or fall, when the soil is usually at maximum moistness and the temperature is moderate enough to allow roots to establish themselves. Timing is less of an issue in warmer regions.

You can purchase balled-and-burlapped trees with roots protected by natural or synthetic burlap material. These plants can be stored in a shady area for a while before planting, as long as you keep the root ball moist. Before planting, pull back the top third of natural burlap and cut any string or twine. Completely remove any synthetic material.

Container trees do not store for quite as long. Once removed from their pot, trees are generally tightly compacted. Using your fingers or a garden tool, gently score the bottom of the root ball to free fine roots from the mass. This way, the roots will expand and grow once planted.

Finally, take care to dig a hole that is three times wider than the diameter of the root ball and no deeper than the tree's original soil. If the hole is too narrow, roots won't expand to anchor the tree. When a hole is too deep, roots cannot access enough oxygen to grow properly. Also, if the tree sinks into the deep hole, water will collect in the low zone at the surface, possibly triggering root rot.

PROTECT TREES **during transportation.**

Plant a Tree

The key to installing trees is preparing a right-sized hole and handling the root ball with care. Think of a root ball as the tree's vital organs. Once planted, they will anchor the tree and work like veins, delivering nutrients and water. Your planting hole should be about three times the diameter of the root ball, but no deeper.

How to Plant a Tree

After preparing the hole, follow these steps for planting a new tree. If your goal is to build a windbreak, place trees far enough apart so the roots can spread. Each tree will have different spreading capacities, so discuss this with a nursery professional or check plant tags for instructions.

1. **Dig the planting hole** and moisten it with water.

2. **Peel back the natural burlap** to expose the top third of the root ball; completely remove any synthetic burlap material. If planting a tree from a container, loosen the fine roots at the bottom of the root ball to promote growth once set into the soil.

3. **Set the tree into the hole,** which should be three times the width of the root ball.

4. **Carefully replace the soil** to backfill around the roots and trunk. Pat the soil with your hands, not your feet. You do not want to compact the soil. You may lay a ring of mulch around the tree to retain moisture.

5. **Deep watering** will ensure that moisture reaches the roots.

PROJECT

TOOLS & MATERIALS

- **Spade**
- **Shovel**
- **Garden tool (for loosening roots)**
- **Backfill soil (combination topsoil, compost, peat moss)**

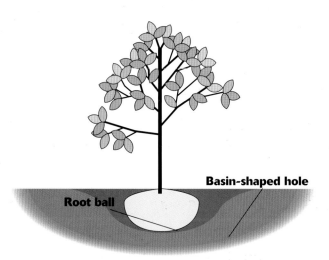

Basin-shaped hole

Root ball

WHEN DIGGING A HOLE to plant a tree, follow this rule of thumb: dig a hole that's roughly three times the diameter of the root ball, but no deeper.

POSITION BARE-ROOT TREES so that the largest branches face southwest. Then spread the roots out in the soil before backfilling the planting hole.

CUT AND REMOVE THE TWINE from the top of balled-and-burlapped trees. Cut the burlap away, and remove it from around the tree.

Pruning Basics

As your trees mature and grow strong on your property, you'll notice unruly shoots or damaged branches that need care. Pruning these is important—it can inspire new growth and prolong the life of trees and shrubs. The entire plant benefits when you remove select portions. Regular pruning also discourages disease and improves the plants' overall appearance.

Timing and technique are critical when pruning. Your pruning technique will, quite literally, mold the future of a shrub or tree. Pinch the ends off of plants for a bushy look. Restore an ornamental's natural shape with some clean-up cuts. Remove rubbing tree branches, where abrasion becomes an open wound for disease to enter. The trick to properly pruning trees and shrubs is to always remember that less is more.

Light, corrective pruning (less than 10 percent of the tree or shrub canopy) can be done all year. But timing is critical when making more severe cuts, such as heading back, thinning, or rejuvenating. Prune when plants are under the least amount of stress. That way, trees and shrubs will heal successfully from wounds that shears and clippers inevitably cause. A plant is stressed when flowering and growing. Late winter and early spring are the best times to conduct severe pruning in most woody plants, flowering trees, and shrubs.

A GAS-POWERED HEDGE TRIMMER lets you control shrubs without cords or recharging time.

Pruning Shrubs

There are several types of pruning, and ideally, you'll use a combination of these methods.

Pinching: The terminal of a shoot is the tip of the stem (the green portion before it becomes woody). The terminal produces a hormone that prevents lateral buds from developing. When you remove the terminal, this hormone-producing bud is lost, allowing lateral buds to grow. Pinching reduces the length of a shoot and promotes filler, or side, growth. Pinch off especially long shoots from inside the shrub canopy.

Heading back: You can increase the density of a shrub by cutting terminal shoots back to a healthy branch or bud. Manipulate the shape of the shrub by cutting inward or outward growing shoots. Be sure that the top bud is located on the side of the branch that faces the direction you want it to grow. For example, an inward-facing bud will develop into a branch that reaches into the canopy. If you allow two opposite-facing buds to grow, the result is a weak, Y-shaped branch. So choose your growth direction, then remove the buds accordingly.

Thinning: Target the oldest, tallest stems first when thinning, which is cutting branches off of the parent stem. (You'll reach into the shrub canopy to accomplish this successfully.) Prune branches that are one-third the diameter of the parent stem. To better visualize where to cut, imagine the Y junction, where a lateral branch meets the parent stem. As with all pruning cuts, practice moderation.

Rejuvenating: Remove the oldest branches by leaving little but a stub near the ground. Young branches can also be cut back, as well as thin stems.

Shearing: Swipe a hedge trimmer over the top of a shrub to remove the terminal of most shoots; this will give you a formal topiary look. Such clean angles must be clipped back throughout the summer to maintain the shape. Shearing is not necessarily beneficial because it forces growth on the exterior of the plant, which blocks light and oxygen from the center. You're left with a shell of a shrub—leaves on the outside, naked branches on the inside.

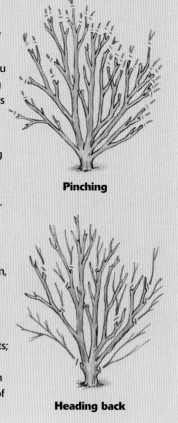

Pinching

Heading back

PROJECT

Trees

Always prune tree branches by cutting just outside the tree collar. You'll notice a circular closure around the wound as the tree begins to heal.

Thinning: These cuts reduce the tree canopy and allow wind to pass through branches. Thinning is a safety measure if you are concerned that a storm will damage a tree and surrounding property. Remove dead, broken, weak, and diseased branches. Cut them back to their point of origin or to laterals that are at least one-third the diameter of the branch you are removing. Be sure to remove less than 25 percent of foliage at one time. It's best to thin trees in the winter, when they are dormant.

Heading back: If your goal is to reduce the size of your tree, cut back lateral branches and heat tips of laterals.

Reduction cut: Most common in younger trees, these cuts remove an offshoot branch back to a thicker branch attached to the tree trunk. Pictured is a cut to remove a perpendicular branch.

TOOLS & MATERIALS

- **Chain saw**
- **Ladder**
- **Safety glasses**

How to Prune a Tree

1. Start by undercutting from beneath the limb with your bow saw or chain saw.

2. Finish the cut from above. This keeps the bark from tearing when the limb breaks loose.

3. Trim the stub from the limb so it's flush with the branch collar.

Avoid digging into a gravel driveway when plowing by attaching skid shoes to front- or rear-mount blades. They come with a pin adjustment so you can set the blade level above the surface.

Snow Removal

Your dream house is ½-mile (.8 km) from the main road, off a gravel road that twists through peaceful woods and careens up and down scenic hillsides. On a spring day, the gravel trek from the main road to the heart of your land offers a true mental escape. But come winter, ice and snow convert this peaceful path into treacherous ground. You can hire someone to clear your driveway, but if you already own a compact utility loader, why not tackle it yourself and save the extra bucks for your heating bill?

Sizing Up the Job

When deciding how to clear snow, first assess the equipment you already have and then discuss with a dealer the various attachments that can get the job done. The scope of your snow-clearing job and your property conditions will dictate the attachment you'll use. For example, a sweeper will gather stones and make a mess if you run it over a gravel driveway. Sweepers are better for paved areas. On the other hand, blades can be adjusted to skim over gravel surfaces. In snowy regions, a bucket will help move snow piles, while a snow thrower will prevent those piles in the first place by tossing snow up and away from the surface being cleared. That way, moving frozen mountains will not become the next chore on your list.

All this considered, you probably already own the necessary equipment to clear snow. Even utility vehicles are capable of pushing snow in lighter-duty applications. Skid steer loaders, which can manage larger land jobs like grading, are virtual power sources that can also carry buckets and blades designed to manage snow. The idea is to put your equipment to work year-round so you can maximize the investment.

Snow Tools

With the right attachments, you can convert your compact utility tractor into a winter crew. Because these vehicles are four-wheel drive, you can ease through snow-covered terrain. To the right are implements that will clear snow from most every surface.

Whenever you add an attachment to your compact utility tractor, be sure the equipment is balanced. You don't want a rear blade to tip your machine onto its back wheels or vice versa. Avoid this by attaching a balance box with 700 or 800 pounds (315 or 360 kg) of weight opposite the attachment. (In this example, fix the balance box on the front of the tractor.) Another alternative if you plan to use a rear-mount blade is to attach a bucket to the front of the tractor, treating this implement as a weight. When using a front-mount blade, rear weights are usually beneficial. Also, you can improve traction by adding weights to your drive tires. Discuss these options with your dealer, who will direct you toward the best choice based on your attachments and power source (tractor). Also, always read the operator's manual for proper equipment and attachment operation and recommended servicing.

TO BLOW OR TO PLOW? A snow-throwing attachment doesn't disturb gravel roads, but takes much longer.

Snow Removal Attachments

Blades: Front-mount blades are most popular, and they range in width up to 66" (167.6 cm). Some features include hydraulic angling so you can adjust how close the blade will skim the surface. Left and right spring-trip mechanisms guard against impact damage. Rear blades attach to a three-point hitch on the back of the utility tractor. The only downside to this setup is that you must crane your neck to see behind the machine during operation.

Bucket: This utility tractor staple is helpful for moving large piles of snow that build up after clearing with a blade.

Snow blower/thrower: For moving excess snow, a snow blower (also called snow thrower) collects snow and blows it out a chute and into the nearby yard. It's the most efficient option, and it will cut through drifts with no trouble. This attachment works equally well on gravel and paved surfaces.

Sweeper: For paved surfaces, a sweeper will brush away light snowfall. But do not use this attachment on gravel driveways. A sweeper brushes over a surface, turning up snow and stones along with it.

Grading the Surface

Changes in grade on your property can introduce runoff problems, resulting in erosion and swampy lowlands that are not conducive to planting, building, or even getting around the land. You can transfer some of the earth from the highlands to these dips and ruts in your property by grading the surface. Depending on the degree of grading necessary, you may wish to contract with a professional who has the heavy-duty equipment required to complete the job. A compact utility tractor with a blade will accomplish light grading jobs. But some cases call for excavators and some expensive iron for moving dirt. Investigate the cost of purchasing the tools to do it yourself versus hiring help. Many homeowners and hobby farmers opt out of this project.

Leveling Land for Drainage

Your home, barn, and other outbuildings should not sit on areas of your property that collect water after a hard rain or snowmelt. Before building, enlist an engineer or a land surveyor who can shoot grades on your property. You'll find out where you need to level the ground. Grading can direct water runoff away from a home, around a barn, and into a drainage swale or creek. Grading is helpful for creating proper irrigation in crop fields. Also, it is a final cleanup step after many land-clearing jobs.

Taming the Topography

Besides grade, examine your property's topography. Are there ditches or sinkholes in an area where you will lay a patio or the foundation for a barn? Do you notice places where water collects in pools? These areas will require special reinforcement when building roads. (See Culverts on page 40.) Are there tree roots, bushes, or other plants you must remove to establish gardens, pastures, roads, or other infrastructure? As you clear the land, you'll find that what's left behind is a surface in need of grading before it can be put to use. Keep in mind: how well you prepare the land will determine the quality of the project you pursue on the land.

Grading for a Patio

As you make improvements to your land, you may want to lay a patio to enjoy the views. This, too, requires knowing the property grade and obtaining the proper slope for adequate drainage. You can compensate for dipping land and sinkholes by building up a slight slope to usher water runoff, or you may excavate land to achieve a flat plane (slightly sloped) on which to lay the patio surface.

Grading a Sloped Yard

Besides grading for drainage purposes, there are aesthetic reasons to level the ground in your back or front yard. A steep slope can botch plans for a patio and outdoor kitchen. And if a patio is constructed on an uneven surface, water runoff can damage outlying areas. There are a couple of solutions. Retaining walls create "steps" and more livable space. You can construct patio space or plant beds on various levels. Or, you may hire a professional to bring in soil and dig out land to create a more even surface. These projects require a bit of math: grading is more than moving dirt. Consult with a professional, and seriously consider hiring out this work.

Determining Grade

While a surveyor can determine the grade of your land, you can estimate the grade of your land before building a patio foundation with a few simple supplies. You'll need two stakes, string, a measuring tape, and a string level. Start by pounding one stake near the foundation of your home. Tie the string to the base of this stake so it is even with the ground. Measure 10 feet (3 m) from this point and pound the second stake into the ground. Attach the string to the second stake, adjusting it to level. Measure the distance between the ground and the string on the second stake. It should be at least 2 inches (5.1 cm) for paved surfaces and 6 inches (15.2 cm) or more for lawns and mulch. (A 10-foot [3-m] distance with a 6-inch distance has a 5 percent grade, which is ideal.) This allowance is enough slope for proper drainage.

A TRANSIT is the most accurate tool for measuring grade.

Any time you grade, you are disturbing the land. Many counties will require a preconstruction meeting before you move dirt, and often a permit is necessary. Review regulations in advance.

BY GRADING AND LEVELING AREAS OF THIS BACKYARD, the contractor built a multilayer patio that serves as an outdoor living room.

CHAPTER 4

Gardens & Growing

A garden of plenty begins with rich, healthy soil that benefits from exposure to sun and water. Timing is everything—where and when you plant root vegetables, vine favorites like tomatoes, and orchard delicacies like raspberries will determine the success of your garden. Your garden skills will improve over time as you sample which edibles grow best on your land. But rather than depending on only trial and error, read up on these foundation skills for preparing and caring for your planted land.

Soil Study

While weather conditions are true variables, the success or failure of our gardening efforts generally lies beneath the surface. Just as you wouldn't expect to run a marathon by fueling your body with junk food, your garden will not reach its potential with soil barren of nutrients. Soil is the support system for garden vegetables, field crops, fruit orchards, and lawns. It provides a balanced meal of phosphorus, potassium, and micronutrients for plants to thrive. Roots depend on soil for nourishment so they can grow deep and strong. Meanwhile, upstairs at ground level, you'll know whether soil is chock full of goodness based on the performance of plants.

Before you start stocking up on seeds and plotting what to include in your backyard salad bowl, assess the quality of your soil. A soil test will help you determine how to prepare the subsurface for planting. There are soil tests designed for different purposes—lawn and garden, horticultural, agronomic—but the process is the same across the board. It all starts with a sample.

Nitrogen is necessary for developing healthy leaf and stem growth.

Recommendations for lawn growth tell you how to improve your soil to support a lawn.

Recommendations for vegetable and flower gardens specify how to amend the soil to foster successful gardens.

Soil texture is classified as one of eleven soil types.

Soil pH measures the acidity or alkalinity of your soil sample.

Potassium promotes flower growth in annuals and perennials.

Phosphorus is needed for strong, healthy root systems.

Soil Test Report

Sample No. 008

Nitrogen (N) (ppm)
20

Soil Texture
Sandy Loam

Soil pH
6.8

Phosphorus (P) (ppm)
15

Potassium (K) (ppm)
125

Nitrogen (N)
Phosphorus (P)
Potassium (K)
Soil PH

Very Low
Low
Medium
High
Very High

Acid   3   4   5   Optimum   6   7   8   Alkaline   9

Recommendations for Home Lawn: The approximate ratio or proportion of these nutrients is: 5-0-5. Apply according to the instructions on the fertilizer bag or container. Since meeting the exact amount required for each nutrient will not be possible in most cases, it is more important to apply the amount of nitrogen required and compromise some for phosphate and potash. Grass clippings left on the lawn is a sound practice.

For Vegetable and Flower Gardens: Manure, compost, or other forms of organic matter may be added. These amendments provide a good source of trace nutrients and improve soil granulation. Three to five bushels of manure or compost per 100 sq. ft. are recommended.

A SOIL TEST REPORT issued by your local agricultural extension service will help you identify any deficiencies in your soil that should be addressed with amendments. A basic lab test costs about $15, and a complete test is generally $25. Test results include an information packet with recommendations on ways to improve soil conditions.

The Elements of Healthy Soil

Whether you test soil in a field or in a trouble spot in your front yard, you're looking for the same basic ingredients to rate its quality. The key elements to examine in a soil test are phosphorus, potassium, and pH level, which is the alkalinity or acidity of the soil. Compare the soil study results to benchmarking averages provided by your county cooperative extension agency. By understanding how your soil stacks up on these three measurements, you have the information you need to determine whether adding fertilizer, compost, lime, or other amendments is necessary.

Additionally, soil tests provide the status of magnesium, cation exchange capacity (CEC), lime requirement index, and base saturation. You can request additional tests for iron, zinc, manganese, soluble salts, and nitrates. Analyzing numbers can be confusing, even for veteran gardeners. Consult with a university extension agent to find out whether levels that do not fall within the average range for your region are cause for concern.

Soil pH

Soil can provide a receptive environment for plant growth if the pH is correct. Soil pH refers to its chemistry: acidic or alkaline. The pH scale runs from 1 (very acidic) to 14 (very alkaline). When soil pH is below 7, it is acidic, and you can face toxicity problems. On the other hand, an alkaline soil with a pH much higher than 7 is probably deficient in nutrients. Ideal soil pH is between 6 and 7. In gardens, certain vegetables like potatoes appreciate more acidic soils with a pH of 6. Turf thrives with a pH of 7 and sometimes a bit higher.

All sorts of variables affect soil pH, including how often you water and fertilize and whether you water too liberally or apply fertilizer with a heavy hand. If soil is too alkaline, you could be dousing your lawn with more water than it needs. If soil is too acidic, you may be overdoing the fertilizer, which is rich in salts that can offset the pH of your soil. The goal always is to strike a pH balance, which is only possible by checking the status of soil so you can make amendments.

If soil test results indicate low pH, the soil probably lacks calcium, magnesium, and potassium. Lime treatments will raise soil pH. There are various products on the market, including hydrated lime granules, or you can replenish nutrients with compost material or even wood ashes. Keep in mind: lime requires waiting two to three months before planting so soil has time to neutralize. Alkaline soils with high pH levels are not as common as acidic soils. Restoring their iron deficiencies requires elemental sulfur. Note: If your pH is high in calcium carbonate, sulfur will not lower the pH level. You can purchase fertilizers that contain sulfate to help balance pH levels. Look for a nitrogen (N), phosphorus (P), potassium (K) rating of 21-3-21. The most dramatic way to change soil pH is to apply sulfur fertilizer forms that contain ammonium. Sulfate will work, but it is slower acting.

ORGANIC AMENDMENTS are the best choice for improving the structure and nutrient levels of your soil. Soil that's been amended properly has a structure that promotes a healthy root system. The roots of these annuals are deep and spread apart.

When testing garden and field areas, draw samples from in between rows to avoid fertilizer bands. In these treated areas, you will not gain a true reading of soil fertility levels.

RICH, HEALTHY SOIL is worth its weight in gold for gardening enthusiasts.

The Dirt on Soil Samples

The primary difference in collecting a soil sample from a yard and a garden is depth. Because you want to test soil quality at the root zone, a 4-inch (10.2 cm) sample from an orchard will not tell the whole story. This depth is just fine for turf, but an apple tree's roots run far deeper. You may need to dig 10 inches (25.4 cm) into the soil under the tree's dripline to take a sample. Typically, field samples are a depth of 6 to 8 inches (15.2 to 20.3 cm), and garden samples should be taken at the depth you are tilling. That will vary depending on what you plant.

When collecting a soil sample, take samples from five to eight spots. Mix them in a pail, then take about a half-cup soil sample from this composite. Send this portion to a lab for testing. When testing a yard with trouble spots, collect soil from good and bad areas, and do not mix them. This way, you can determine deficiencies in weak areas. Also, keep in mind the geography of a field. If a portion of your crop grows on a slope, collect a separate batch of soil samples from this area rather than the low-lying portion of your property that is seemingly more fertile.

Collect Soil for Testing

Take care when collecting soil samples to send into an extension service for testing. What are your goals? If you want to manage nutrient deficiency in a dry spot but the rest of the lawn is healthy, you'll draw samples from the dry spot and package them separately from the healthy soil. To evaluate your property's soil content, take samples from different areas and mix them together. These steps will help you through the process.

TOOLS & MATERIALS

- **Soil probe, auger, garden trowel, or spade**
- **Clean plastic pail or box**
- **Zipper-plastic bag**
- **Soil test order form from lab**

How to Collect Soil for Testing

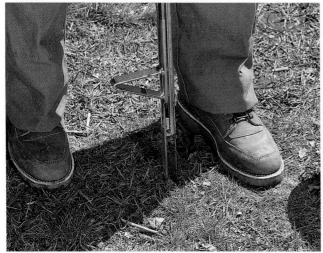

1. Collect soil cores. Remove any top debris from the surface, and use a shovel or small soil probe to randomly collect up to 10 samples that are about $3/4$" in diameter. Each sample should be taken from the same depth and volume.

2. Mix soil. Combine cores in a clean plastic (not metal) bucket. Thoroughl move enough to fill a plastic bag. Laboratories often provide sample bags for this purpose.

3. Prepare the sample by loading the specified amount of soil into the container or bag provided by the soil testing laboratory. Complete the lab order form, indicating which plants you intend to grow. Check boxes to order a basic or complete test. A basic test will provide your soil pH level and all other information you need to determine whether your soil needs amendments.

Too Much?

What happens when soil contains excessive levels of potassium, phosphorus, or nitrogen?

Potassium: Elevated potassium levels in forage crops can be detrimental to animal health.

Phosphorous: Too much phosphorus combined with surface water runoff can cause plants and algae in surface waters to grow in excess, therefore damaging aquatic ecosystems.

Nitrogen: Nitrogen boosts growth rate, but too much of this good thing results in overgrowth of forage and underperformance of the bounty, whether flowers or tomatoes.

FOR SOME, THE METHODICAL CHORE of tilling fields is a relaxing escape and an enjoyable way to spend hours on the land.

Tilling & Amending Soil

The best soil for growing is slightly acidic, well draining, and rich with organic matter. Most unimproved land doesn't naturally meet this ideal, but with some tilling and amending most soils can be readied for planting.

Sandy soil acts like a strainer, allowing water and nutrients to pass right through it. Deep-root watering becomes a challenge when soil does not retain moisture long enough for plants to drink it up. Clay soils stay too wet, suffer from compaction issues, and therefore do not contain the oxygen that plant root systems require. Your

goal is a happy medium. A soil that is equal parts clay, sand, and organic matter will not allow nutrients to leach or filter through soil without enriching it.

The good news is you can manipulate your soil profile by using amendments to balance the structure so it is ideal for planting. Also, with information gathered from a soil pH test, you can improve soil fertility. By managing soil profile and nutrient levels, you will pave the way for your garden vegetables and crops to succeed.

Soil Preparation

To amend and prepare soil for planting, first till or plow the land. The size of your planting space will dictate the method required to churn up soil so you can blend in amendments and nutrients and loosen particles to make room for seed. Hand till a home garden by double-digging the space, or use a rototiller machine to perform the hard labor. Fields require a compact utility tractor with plow and rake. You may wish to contract out extensive tillage—say 40 acres or more.

Fall is an ideal time to till garden beds. Plowed fields allow for earlier planting in the spring, and the winter cold will kill insects and weeds that are churned up and buried by the soil. Freezing and thawing action also helps break up compact soils. If you lay down manure, wood ash, limestone, or other insoluble fertilizers in the fall, they settle and break down into the soil over the winter. When applied in spring or during the growing season, the toxicity of these elements can shock and damage plants.

There are instances when spring is the better tilling time. For one, avoid fall plowing or tilling in areas prone to erosion, unless you want to exacerbate the problem by exposing soil for months. Also, if you choose to grow a cover crop, which becomes "green manure" when turned over in spring, you'll plant in fall rather than till/plow. (See Cover Crops on page 92.) If you till in the fall, you will still level and rake soil in the spring to prepare an even surface for planting.

Ask the Extension Service

One of your most valuable references as you prepare your land for planting is your local cooperative extension service. These offices are housed at land-grant universities, and every U.S. state and territory has an extension office. For instance, Ohio's extension service is housed at Ohio State University. When you call a cooperative extension office, you will reach experts who can provide research-based answers to your questions about anything from soil quality to hardy crops for your region. Need to have a soil sample analyzed? Your extension service can manage this and provide instruction to help you improve the quality of your soil. (Refer back to Soil Study on page 84.) Keep the phone number of your local extension on hand. Offices may host events and educational seminars, open to the public.

The United States Department of Agriculture Cooperative State Research, Education, and Extension Service (CSREES) is a national non-credit educational network, and you can search for local extension offices through this organization. For more information, log on to www.csrees.usda.gov. The CSREES provides federal funding to the cooperative extension system, which includes offices in every state.

The Jar Test

You can tell what type of soil you're working with by conducting a jar test. Fill a quart jar two-thirds full with water. Gradually add to the jar a soil sample from the desired planting area. Continue adding soil until water reaches the top of the jar. Cover and shake, then allow the sediment to settle for a day. The sand will settle first, then silt, and finally clay. Is your soil predominantly sand? Mostly clay? This will help you determine which amendments are necessary to establish a balanced soil structure. Depending on your jar test results, you can amend your soil to create fertile ground for planting. Soil with high clay content requires adding a combination of sand, silt, clay, minerals, and organic matter to amend the soil and improve its consistency. Sandy soil needs improved water retention so roots have an opportunity to soak in moisture before it escapes. You can improve soil body by working in topsoil and organic matter.

When digging out turf to create a garden bed, set aside some sod pieces and use them to patch trouble spots in your lawn. You can compost the leftovers.

Tilling

Before digging, be sure soil conditions are appropriate for tilling. If you can squeeze soil into a ball, it's too wet. Soil is too dry if it looks powdery or clumpy. If it crumbles and falls freely from your hand, it's just right.

Next, be sure you have the right tools for the job. For tilling fields, rely on a workhorse like a utility tractor (compact or full-sized, depending on the size of your job). The multistep process begins with plowing to break up the soil surface. This digging action mixes up vegetation and creates a welcome medium for applying fertilizer or lime. Next, a rake attachment works to harrow fields, which smoothes the surface for planting. With tilling, less is more. Machines put pressure on fields, compacting soil with their weight. While you can't plow a field without equipment, take care to do so moderately.

For tilling a garden bed, use a skid steer loader with attachments in the smaller space and perform the same process you would in a larger field. Or rely on a rototiller. These machines fluff up the top layer of beds with their rotating tines. The downside to rototilling is that below tine level, soil becomes compacted and slick, forming what master gardeners refer to as a hardpan. This subsurface prevents deep-growing roots from maturing.

Double-Digging Beds

Hard labor pays off in the garden, and double-digging beds certainly will test your endurance. Your reward is the quality and yield of kitchen herbs and vegetables your garden will produce. This age-old process is only necessary every few years, and it requires a spade, shovel, garden fork, wheelbarrow, and amendments

A ROTOTILLER is a convenient tool for tilling smaller gardens and planting beds, but it is not intended for large tracts of land.

like peat and compost. Systematically dig out rows of soil, churning up the subsurface with a fork and mixing in peat and compost. (You can also use manure, wood ash, lime, or other inorganic fertilizers indicated by your soil pH test.)

Double-digging is practical for small gardens. First, use a spade to dig a row about 2 feet (61 cm) wide. Shovel this dirt into your wheelbarrow. (You'll use it later.) Next, fork over the subsoil to the depth of the fork prongs. During this time, mix in organic material. Move to the next row and repeat the spade process. Shovel the second row's dirt on top of the first completed row. Fork over subsoil of the second row, mixing in organic material. Now, move to the third row, and continue the pattern. Use the reserved soil from the first row to fill your last row.

Soil Amendments

Double-digging, tilling, and plowing prepare the ground to accept soil conditioners, which improve soil aeration, drainage, moisture retention, and tilth (soil workability). Remember the jar test? Mixing in organic products like peat moss, sawdust, wood chips, and perlite can change the structure of too-sandy or overly compacted soils.

Additionally, a soil pH test may indicate that soil is too acidic or alkaline. Dolomitic limestone adds calcium and magnesium, increasing soil pH. (Remember, lower pH levels are more acidic, higher pH levels are more alkaline.) Elemental sulfur acidifies alkaline soil. Wood ash can be used instead of limestone, but be sure to spread this in the winter so it incorporates into soil. Practice moderation with wood ash. It is actually quite toxic to plants when applied in excess. Limit applications to no more than 20 pounds. (9 kg) per 1,000 square feet (92.9 sq. m).

Other soil nutrients you may add include greensand and granite meal for potassium. Cottonseed meal, kelp meal, bone meal, leather meal, and worm castings also help fertilize soil. If you raise animals like horses, sheep, rabbits, or poultry, their manure can be applied in fall and tilled into the soil. Manure is high in nitrogen, so if applied during the growing season, it may burn plants. Composted manure is less potent and can be applied during the season to nonedible crops and turf.

By relying on organic materials to improve soil profile and nutrient content, you can reduce the need for synthetic fertilizers. Also, you can farm sustainably by recycling grass clippings and other compostable greens and browns into beneficial soil builders.

Leaves

Grass

Peat moss

Compost

Straw

Manure

Cover Crops

Cover crops represent an integral component of sustainable farming and gardening practices. Planting soybeans, oats, alfalfa, rye, and other off-season seeds will feed the soil with nutrients all winter long. Meanwhile, cover crops prevent erosion, and plant roots act like diggers, loosening compacted, subsurface hardpan. You'll notice improved soil workability without the use of synthetic fertilizers. Because the cost of fertilizers has increased in recent years, more landowners are exploring this natural approach. Many landowners are also realizing the environmental benefits of adopting a more natural approach to farming.

Cover crops are not intended for feed or sale. Essentially, they're between-season fillers. They protect a garden or field during winter and improve soil fertility so land is ready to plant in spring. Plow, till, and turn up the young crop, feeding the earth with what is called green manure. Legume crops are especially rich in nitrogen, which reduces the need for fertilizers. After all, nitrogen is the primary ingredient in synthetic fertilizers. Legume cover crops include clover, hairy vetch, field pea, annual medic, alfalfa, and soybean.

Nonlegume crops recycle soil nitrogen and reduce leaching of nutrients. For soil that is already rich in nitrogen, these crops are ideal winter covers because they will retain all that good stuff contained in the soil. Nonlegumes include rye, oat, wheat, forage turnip, oilseed radish, and buckwheat.

The best time to plant cover crops is one month before the first killing frost. If you grow fall vegetables, you can still plant cover crop seeds in between rows. Same goes for fields. Turn up the cover crop so it becomes green manure at least two weeks before planting vegetables. Turn the crop over before it grows too tall, but you want it to stay in the ground as long as possible in the spring so soil can benefit from additional nutrients. It will also help suppress spring weeds.

A THREE-YEAR ROTATION of corn, soybean, and wheat (pictured at right) can improve crop yield.

ALFALFA is a deep-rooted perennial plant from the pea family. It has small divided leaves, purple cloverlike flowers, and spiral pods that are used extensively for fodder and pasture and as a cover crop.

SOYBEANS are annual crop plants, also from the pea family. They are native to China and Japan, but widely grown for its seeds, which are rich in protein and oil. Soybeans are used as a forage and cover crop.

GENERATIONS HAVE USED ANNUAL RYEGRASS for forage. As a cover crop, ryegrass can grow more than 5 feet, creating a pathway for corn and soybean, and it helps rebuild soil through deep-rooting.

Compost Clinic

Compost is a natural digestion process by which microorganisms break down organic materials into base components that encourage new plant growth. Microorganisms are bacteria, fungi, worms, and insects. In the right conditions, microorganisms efficiently convert compost materials into humus. This is a loamy, nutrient-rich soil. Composted materials enrich gardens, fields, and landscape plant beds. Recycle grass clippings, leaves, manure, and even kitchen scraps by composting these ingredients into beneficial food for your soil.

Compost Conditions

Air, water, temperature, and food dictate the speed at which compost material will break down. The difference between managed and passive composting is speed, which requires your active participation. If you are not in a hurry, you can set up a compost pile or fill a bin, and just wait. After a year or two, add clippings or leaves to the pile and the material will eventually compost. But if you want to prompt nature into the express lane, you'll need a balance of carbon and

YOU CAN COMPOST MATERIAL in bins. You can construct your own by using reclaimed wood.

nitrogen, the right temperature, and good air and water circulation. Increase your yield each season by mixing and chopping materials and monitoring conditions in your compost pile. You should be able to produce several batches of humus.

Air

The microbes that decompose compost materials are aerobic. They're active. Air gives them breathing room; without it, microbes basically shut down and allow their anaerobic cousins to take over the pile. Anaerobic microbes thrive with little oxygen and will slow down decomposition. Plus, they smell like garbage. Healthy, aerobic microbes will not diffuse an odor you may associate with compost. An active, well-balanced compost pile produces material that smells like soil in your backyard.

For the best air circulation, ensure that air passageways in your compost pile are not blocked by combining heavier ingredients, such as grass clippings or wet leaves, with materials that allow air to penetrate, such as straw. Create layers of different textured materials, and turn the pile periodically to promote air circulation. Do this by using a garden fork or spade to break apart the pile, and "fluff" it by restacking the pile.

AIR IS AN ESSENTIAL INGREDIENT in the composting process. Turn the pile occasionally to discourage matting and clumping.

Water

A dry compost pile will delay the decomposition process. A wet pile chokes out air circulation. Ideally, compost should be damp like a wrung-out sponge. It should be coated, but not drenched, in water. That said, if you want to add dry leaves or grass clippings to your compost pile, wet them with a hose as you add them in layers. But beware of too much wetness. Soggy kitchen scraps or heavy, green grass clippings will need to dry out a bit to prevent weighing down your compost pile with excess moisture.

Temperature

Track the temperature of your compost pile to be sure the material is warm. By simply feeling the inside of the pile, you can detect coolness, which means outside air is inhibiting microbial activity. Purchase a compost thermometer at a garden store, and aim for a constant temperature between 104 and 130 degrees Fahrenheit (40 to 54 degrees Celsius). At this temperature, the pile is at its peak. Hotter piles decompose faster.

A COMPOST THERMOMETER lets you monitor the progress of the composting and helps alert you if there is a problem.

COLLECT MANURE FROM AROUND THE FARM on a regular basis (left photo), and transport it to a designated area for composting (right photo). For obvious reasons, the designated area should be out of the way and downwind from your farmhouse, if possible.

Composting Manure

The same elements of composting apply to manure, but you should consider these potential risks when applying manure to food gardens. First, do not put manure from dogs, cats, and pigs in your food garden. Second, if you apply manure to a garden within 60 days of harvest, it must be aged for at least a year or hot composted. Fresh manure should never be applied after a garden is planted due to potential pathogens that may contaminate food. Cover manure piles with a tarp to prevent them from drying out in summer or becoming too soggy in the winter. Turn the piles over regularly so the heat from the core of the piles will kill parasites and weed seeds on the outside material. If weed seeds develop, your pile may not be large enough to generate the necessary heat. Composting can occur as quickly as a few weeks or take up to three months, depending on conditions.

Browns and Greens

Just as humans need a balance of nutrients for energy, so does a fast-burning compost pile. Compost consists of browns or greens. Browns are high in carbon, which is food energy that microorganisms depend on to decompose the pile. Greens are high in nitrogen, which is a protein source for the multiplying microbes. A ratio of 3-to-1 brown-to-green materials is the best balance.

Browns
- **Dry brown plant material**
- **Dry brown weeds**
- **Wood chips**
- **Straw**
- **Sawdust**

Greens
- **Grass clippings**
- **Kitchen fruit and vegetable scraps**
- **Green leaves**
- **Manure**

WHETHER YOUR ENTIRE ESTATE IS LAWN or just the areas around your main residence, maintaining lush, green grass takes plenty of effort and input.

Your Lawn Care Program

Your lawn may consume a modest portion of your property. Or perhaps you have chosen not to raise crops or animals on your land and therefore treat your great estate like rolling acres of sports turf, every bit of it neatly trimmed and perfectly green. Regardless, there is an area on your land that demands more attention than, say, a wildflower field or a grazing pasture. Because we often encourage grass to grow in challenging conditions, it needs extra nutrients to achieve the color, density, and longevity we expect. This is where your lawn care program comes into play.

A proper lawn care program promotes the growth of healthy grass while managing weeds, insects, and disease.

It includes fertilizer, herbicides, and, when needed, products to prevent or control insects and pests. Lawn care programs differ based on region and turf type. You may choose to hire a professional to care for your yard as you focus on the garden and other projects that interest you. If lawn care is one of those projects, first consult with your cooperative extension agency and determine your turfgrass type. Understand the physical characteristics your turfgrass should display when healthy. Familiarize yourself with its response to air temperature (the season) and moisture. These conditions are the basis of your fertilization and weed-control program.

Fertilizers

The methods and products you employ for nourishing crop fields and gardens are quite different from a fertilization program for turf. Most likely, you will incorporate compost and other organic substances into areas where you grow food. You can use foliar fertilizer sparingly in the garden to promote plant health. Large crop fields are extremely expensive to fertilize, and therefore synthetics are a last resort for hobby farmers. But in the lawn, a regular fertilizer program is one of the most effective ways to maintain a healthy, lush, and appealing yard.

Fertilizer is composed of nitrogen, phosphorus, and potassium (N, P, and K), and you will find the ratio of these three elements listed in that order on every product package. If a label reads 1-2-1, it contains one part nitrogen, two parts phosphorus, and one part potassium. Depending on the ratio of these elements, fertilizer will help turf look greener, grow faster, or wear longer. Your goal is to strike a balance.

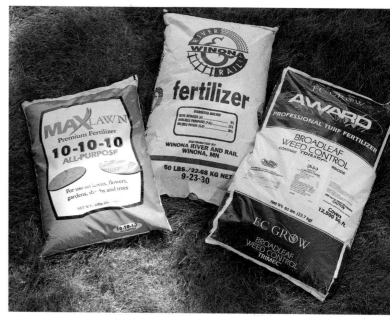

BUILDING CENTERS, YARD AND GARDEN CENTERS, hardware stores, and agricultural supply stores all carry a large inventory of fertilizer products for various conditions and purposes.

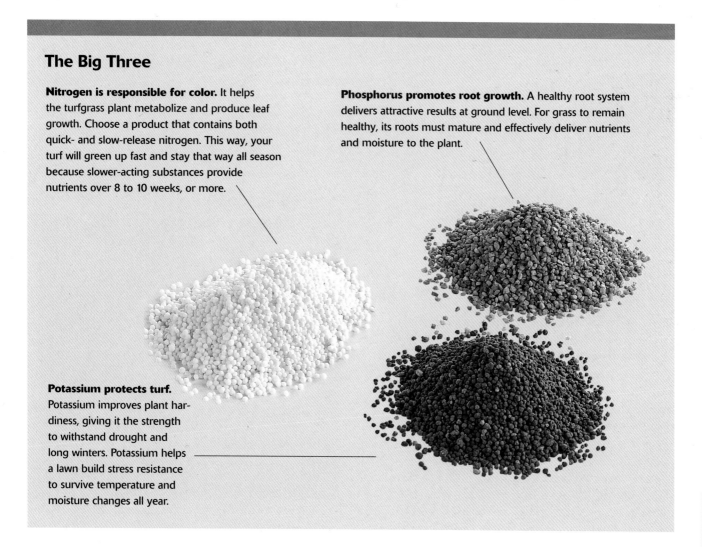

The Big Three

Nitrogen is responsible for color. It helps the turfgrass plant metabolize and produce leaf growth. Choose a product that contains both quick- and slow-release nitrogen. This way, your turf will green up fast and stay that way all season because slower-acting substances provide nutrients over 8 to 10 weeks, or more.

Phosphorus promotes root growth. A healthy root system delivers attractive results at ground level. For grass to remain healthy, its roots must mature and effectively deliver nutrients and moisture to the plant.

Potassium protects turf. Potassium improves plant hardiness, giving it the strength to withstand drought and long winters. Potassium helps a lawn build stress resistance to survive temperature and moisture changes all year.

CHEMICAL HERBICIDES should be used judiciously, and great care should be taken to follow the application instructions. Choosing the best product can get tricky: there is no such thing as a one-size-fits-all weed killer.

Herbicides

Dandelions probably aren't the flowers you had in mind for your property, especially in the portion dedicated to the lawn. Control broadleaf weeds, along with other unwanteds like crabgrass, with herbicide applications. You can buy products called weed-and-feed, also identified as preemergence/fertilizer blends. These granular formulas are a two-for-one special for your grass. Preemergence means the herbicide controls weeds before they sprout, creating a barrier of protection. Preemergence herbicides should be applied to a lawn in early spring. Postemergence herbicides knock down weeds that have already sprouted. Spray problem areas with a liquid product. Timing for both herbicide types depends on your grass type. This is why it's a good idea to get advice from a professional. A licensed lawn care operator can best diagnose and recommend an individualized turf treatment program for insect and disease problems.

Selective herbicides: knock down weed species without affecting growth of other plants; safe for application on healthy turf.

Nonselective herbicides: eliminate weeds and anything else growing in the area, including your grass. Ideal for killing large turf areas that will be renovated into a landscape bed.

Contact herbicides: spot treatments that affect only the area touched by the herbicide.

Systemic herbicides: slow-acting weed control for turf, delivered through the plant's vascular system.

WEARING PROTECTIVE CLOTHING AND GEAR, apply weed killer to the affected areas.

Professional Lawn Care Services

Need a little help maintaining your lawn? A large plot of land requires a lot of attention and sometimes that work can just be too much, especially if you go on vacation.

So, to whom do you turn for help? Professional lawn service companies cover the full range of treatments and maintenance tasks for turfgrass (as the fussy green stuff is known among experts). There are two basic levels of professional lawn service: treatment services and complete lawn care. Which level is right for you may be directly related to how much those dandelion roots have broken your spirit.

Lawn care service: The core function of lawn treatment services is to spray your grass with chemicals to control weeds, insects, and disease and to apply fertilizers to make the lawn thick and green. The rest of the work—watering, mowing, and general maintenance—is your responsibility. And it's important to keep your end of the bargain, because inadequate care between professional treatments will render them useless (unless you just enjoy having a fresh coating of chemicals on your property).

Complete maintenance: Full-service lawn care can be like having your own groundskeeper. Mowing, trimming, fertilizing, and tree and shrub care are blissfully whisked from your weekly schedule, leaving you time for more noble pursuits, like laundry or cleaning out the garage. Many service providers also take care of occasional lawn treatments, including power raking, aeration, and sprinkler system service. In snowy climates, companies may also contract for snow removal.

Choosing landscape service: Before selecting a landscape company for maintenance or lawn care applications, talk with several candidates about their application programs and techniques. You'll want to know what type of products are used, how often they are applied, and the company's general philosophy on treating weeds and disease. Some companies advertise organic, or "healthy," lawn care treatments. Do your homework and find out if this is truly the case. The only real organic form of lawn care is improving soil nutrition and turf health to avoid disease and weeds in the first place—in the pest control world, they adopt a practice called "IPM," or Integrated Pest Management. It promotes prevention instead of mere curative treatment. (Learn more about natural turf care on page 107.)

Obtain price quotes from several companies and check references. All quotes should include a detailed schedule of services and treatments proposed for your lawn. Ask about the companies' experience and training, and find out if they are certified by organizations

WHEN YOU FIRST MOVED onto your hobby farm, hiring a professional lawn care service may have been the furthest thing from your mind. But lawn care is not for everyone, and you may find that you're much happier leaving this task to others.

like PLANET, the Professional Landcare Network (www.landcarenetwork.com). Don't make your decision based on price. Rather, focus on the professionals' experience working with lawns in your area and their track record for keeping customers happy.

Licenses & insurance: The most important license held by lawn service providers is for pesticide use. Most states require certification and licensure for anyone who applies pesticides (including insecticides, herbicides, and fungicides). Make sure your contractor has the required training and credentials. Lawn service companies should be insured for liability and workers' compensation. Lawn services have been known to spread diseases with contaminated chemicals, so make sure they have insurance to repair any damage they might cause.

Application Basics

Depending on the size of your lawn, the tools you'll rely on for applying lawn care products range from a basic walk-behind broadcast spreader to attachments that tow behind riding lawn mowers and heavy-duty implements designed for utility tractors. You can cover more area faster with a vehicle and attachment, but your lawn may consume just a fraction of your property. In such a case, a manual tool like the one pictured here works just fine.

Lawn care application is a science that involves careful product selection, calibration of equipment, and attention to labels that contain chemistry symbols you may not have seen since high school. Starting with the N-P-K rating (that's nitrogen, phosphorus, potassium), you will choose a formula with a ratio that will accomplish your goals. Refer to the previous section on how N, P, and K work in fertilizers, or consult with a licensed lawn care operator, who can design an appropriate program for your lawn.

Also on the label are instructions on how much product to apply, a laundry list of active ingredients, and safe-usage instructions. Treat the label as law. Wear recommended safety gear, such as eye protection, and manage spills as directed on packaging.

Granular or Liquid?

The fertilizer and weed-and-feed products designed for the whole lawn will probably be granular products. They are more cost-effective and can be applied over large areas with a broadcast spreader. Granular fertilizers work by entering turf plants through the root system. Granules are timed-release, and they can be applied less frequently than liquid applications. The downside is that some of the product is absorbed by soil as it leaches down to the plant root zone.

Liquids are ideal for spot-treating areas with weeds. Leaves absorb the product and transfer active ingredients to roots. You'll get quick results but risk dilution of the product after a heavy rain. Purchase herbicides in spray bottle form for fast knockdown in trouble spots.

DROP SPREADERS WORK by releasing fertilizer directly from the hopper onto the turf in an even, defined path. When using a drop spreader, be sure to overlap each pass to avoid striping later on—a sure sign that you missed a spot.

WHEN OPERATING a drop spreader, always overlap passes. Line up the center of the spreader to the center of your last wheel track.

THE BEST WAY TO APPLY granular fertilizer accurately is to divide the application in half. Apply the first half in one direction, then apply the second half in a path perpendicular to your first pass. So, if you wheel the spreader toward your home on the first pass, for example, work toward your neighbor's house on the second round. A double pass method will prevent striping patterns that can result when you miss a spot.

BROADCAST SPREADERS are adjustable so you can match the rate of coverage recommended for the product you're dispensing.

FERTILIZER BAGS list spreader settings, so check those recommendations before calibrating your spreader.

Even Coverage

The trick to covering ground with a fertilizer application without burning out your lawn is proper calibration. Calibration is the process of setting your spreader to distribute granules at the rate given by the usage instructions on the product label. (Did you read the label?) Follow these steps to calibrate your walk-behind broadcast spreader.

Measure your lawn: Use a wheel measure or step off the length and width for a size estimate.

Determine product requirement: Based on your property size, purchase enough bags to cover the area. The label will indicate how much square footage (square meters) a bag of product will cover.

Check label for calibration setting: Settings may be listed in letters or numbers. For example, set spreader on E or 5. If the bag indicates a letter setting and your equipment has number settings, simply count a number for every letter in the alphabet to get the appropriate setting. (E and 5 are the same setting.)

You're set to spread: Divide product in half and apply in two passes. If your property requires six bags of fertilizer, pour half of this in the spreader. If you wheel toward your home on the first pass, work toward your neighbor's house with the second half of your application.

ACCOMMODATING A GROWING DEMAND for organic produce, some farmers focus on sustainable practices so they can market their goods to green-minded customers.

Organic Options

A trip down practically any grocery produce aisle will reveal a growing trend in U.S. agriculture. Do you reach for just a head of cabbage or for the certified organic cabbage that carries a premium price? Will you bypass the superstore and shop local farmers' markets, where the produce doesn't travel by way of gas-guzzling trucks or planes from out-of-state or faraway lands? Are you looking more closely at labels? If so, you're not alone.

Why Go Organic?

Since 1997, organic food sales have shown annual growth rates of 15 to 21 percent, according to the Organic Trade Association.

Organically farmed produce is cultivated without chemicals and grown on land maintained by using sustainable practices. Those include: incorporating peat and composted manure into vegetable beds; relying on tilling rather than spraying herbicides; and allowing beneficial insects and earthworms to do their work on the land without our intervention.

Organic practices apply not just to vegetable gardening and raising field crops, but also to lawn care. In turf maintenance, the focus is on proper mowing practices, irrigation, and fertilization with natural products that enhance the soil's biotic quality and encourage microbial activity. That's the type of action you want to take place in soil so it remains balanced and ripe with nutrients—a combination that welcomes planting of all kinds, whether turf or root vegetables.

Landowners choose to adopt organic growing practices for various reasons. Those who produce a bounty of vegetables to sell may find success in targeting customers who seek out "farm-fresh" organic produce. Other property owners prefer organic turf care practices because they are conscious of how certain fertilizer and weed control products may affect animals, whether cows or the family dog. Let's examine some ways you can incorporate organic practices on the lawn, field, and in the garden.

VEGETABLES GROWN without the use of synthetic fertilizers and herbicides leave a better taste in your mouth.

IF YOU DEPEND ON THE NATURAL RESOURCES that are available for free on your land, you will be well on your way to becoming an organic farmer. In addition to composting animal manure, marshy grasses can be harvested and used as bed mulch over the winter.

THE CERTIFIED ORGANIC LABEL has more importance from a consumer standpoint than a grower standpoint—it is a question of what kind of food you wish to feed your family. As a hobby farmer, however, if you grow and sell more than $5,000 of produce per year, you should become familiar with the qualifications.

Farm to Fork

How rewarding would it be to pick a blueberry from your backyard and pop the tart fruit right in your mouth—no washing? What about pulling a carrot out of the garden and rinsing it without concern that it should be cooked "just in case"? And you can forget any poison warning signs at your garden gate if your produce is organically grown.

But what does that mean? The USDA's National Organic Program spells out standards for farmers who wish to adopt the certified seal for produce they sell. Farmers who sell more than $5,000 in organic produce each year must be certified if they wish to use the label. You likely are growing as a hobby, and certification is not necessary; it's voluntary. If you want to call yourself organic, you must follow the rules and keep records. Currently, there is a fair amount of disagreement among small local producers and large agricultural operations about the certified organic designation and who may use it. Unless you are selling product for profit you needn't be concerned about it, but as a consumer you may have

an interest. It is also important to get up to speed with the differences among locally grown, sustainably grown, and organically grown.

Organic Standards

You can learn more about the type of records you must maintain and the required farming practices by reviewing official government standards on organic practices. You'll learn that you must document your production methods, as well as how you harvest and handle all produce. A farm plan is part of the certification process, and it must address how you deal with weed and pest problems, your compost practices, and other land care details. For example, organic produce cannot be labeled as such until the farm is free of prohibited substances for three years; and raw manure must be composted before it is used on land where food crops grow. Hobby farmers will discover that abiding by organic growing standards fulfills their goal of caring for their property and being conscientious stewards of the land.

Follow the one-third rule when mowing. Never remove more than one-third of a blade of grass at one time. If turf is 6" (15.2 cm) long, remove 2" (5.1 cm) in a single cut.

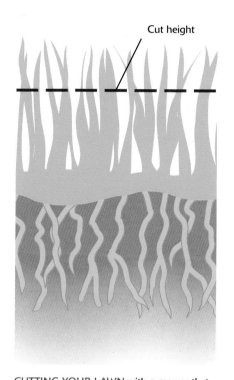

Cut height

CUTTING YOUR LAWN with a mower that mulches not only saves you the time and effort of bagging, it also returns the clipped grass into the lawn where the nutrients will feed the living grass plants as the cut ends decompose.

Natural Turf Care

Prevention is the key word in organic lawn care. Soil can be improved with organic matter, fertilizer can be applied less frequently—and that fertilizer does not need to contain synthetic materials. You can recycle weeds and organic and animal waste by composting, then feeding that goodness back to the land.

But what about the golf course–green lawn? Well, you don't have to give up your lush lawn if you decide to go organic. Actually, the opposite is true if you start at the root of turf health, which is the soil. We discussed in detail the components of healthy soil for gardens, and the same holds true for turf. Get a soil test, find out what elements are missing, and focus on establishing a healthy foundation for your yard.

Besides soil nutrition, following are some other best practices to consider if you want to pursue a natural lawn care program. For more details, consult with a county extension agent or inquire about natural lawn care service providers in your community. This niche has also expanded along with the public's sharpened awareness of turf management.

Mowing: Organic lawns are mowed higher. Longer turf protects soil, prevents weed seed germination, and reduces water loss.

Watering: Choose more drought-tolerant turf types, such as tall fescue, Kentucky bluegrass, and perennial ryegrass. Water early in the morning so soil can absorb moisture.

Fertilizing: Opt for organic fertilizers derived from animal manures and plant sources, such as alfalfa meal and cottonseed meal. Always read labels because some organic products are enhanced with synthetic chemicals.

Build a Garden

Don't allow the traditional rectangular-shaped garden box you into a garden design. The plot you choose for cultivating vegetables, herbs, and flowers may fit into a nook of any form near your home, provided it is the recipient of abundant sunlight. You may clear a spot for a pie-shaped herb garden that holds all the ingredients you need to flavor a savory batch of tomato sauce. Of course, practicality should rule as you build your garden with attention to location, size, and row arrangement. Consider the possibilities, but before you break ground, focus on how you will use the garden every day.

Keep the location of your farmhouse in mind when planning a vegetable garden. Not only is a lavish garden in full bloom a beautiful sight out of your window, it is nice to have a nearby resource for a handful of greens or a couple of tomatoes just a few steps away. Locating the garden in easy sight also lets you keep an eye out for uninvited diners.

Before you select a spot for your garden, take time to test soil pH and determine soil content. You may discover that the plot you thought would be the perfect place for growing vegetables would be a better place for a rock garden because the soil is simply not prepared for planting. Remember, soil quality and sun exposure control the success of your garden. Fortunately, you can manipulate these variables by amending soil and choosing the right plant for the right place. Whether you choose to build raised beds, plant large fields of vegetables, or section off a small pie-shaped spot for an herb garden, the same soil rules apply.

Before you get soil into shape for planting, choose a design for your bed. There are functional rectangle beds, raised beds, and herb gardens arranged in squares or planted in a wheel. You can even carve out amoeba-shaped flower beds for curb appeal. There really are no strict boundaries for gardens. But before you decide to do all of the above, get out a pencil and paper and sketch a picture of your property. Draw in your farm house, barn or shed, roads, and other infrastructure you must work around. Now, outline where you will grow your bounty. Visualizing how your garden will appear in the larger scheme of things can help you decide what type of beds are best for your land.

ENTICING ROWS OF VEGETABLES keep an avid gardener busy during the growing season.

YOU CAN USE A HOSE OR ROPE to layout potential garden bed shapes and sizes before you begin stripping off turf.

Bed Design

Function is the driver for farmers who choose oblong gardens with neatly organized rows. Rectangles are more sensible for using machinery to till—longer rows with just enough space between them for tractor wheels to tread. This formation is convenient for quaint vegetable gardens that are too small for mechanized labor, as well as half-acre plots that contain a sampling of field crops, such as corn.

Regardless of the size of your garden, design it in a geometrical shape (square, rectangle, pie-shaped for herbs) that allows you to divide it into workable sections you can access easily. Following are some considerations as you determine the layout of your garden bed.

Plant selection: Make a list of what you will plant in your garden. You may decide to create several separate gardens that house various types of plants—herbs, cutting flowers, root vegetables. Or mix and match these categories in one space, keeping in mind that certain plants complement each other. Other flowers, such as buddleia, attract butterflies. Do your plant research first, then determine the logistics of your bed.

Water source: Consider areas on your property with easy access to a water source.

Location: Tune in to the elements: wind, water, sun. Review your plant list and choose a site accordingly. Cool-season veggies like carrots will perform in shade; but peppers and tomatoes need full sun. For the most part, gardens need a good six hours of sunlight each day to thrive. Also take into account topography: avoid planting on steep slopes, which will introduce puddling and erosion problems unless you terrace the area.

Tools: You'll readily use a wheelbarrow to collect weeds or harvest your bounty. Perhaps you will till your row crops with a compact utility tractor. Consider what equipment must fit in between your garden rows for you to care for your plants. When planting, you must make room.

Paths: Paths should be close enough together that your legs can straddle a bed. They should be wide enough for a wheelbarrow to pass through. Prepare paths that are friendly to foot traffic by laying down mulch or wood chips or planting grass.

Build raised bed borders with pressure-treated lumber, redwood, cement block, or brick. Cement block can raise soil pH over time. Avoid lumber that's treated with creosote, pentachlorophenol, or chromated copper arsenic (CCA). These are hazardous chemicals that can leach into the soil.

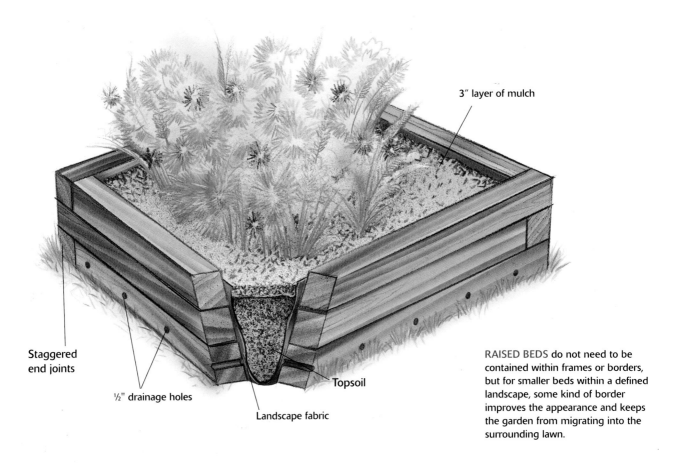

3″ layer of mulch

Staggered end joints

½″ drainage holes

Topsoil

Landscape fabric

RAISED BEDS do not need to be contained within frames or borders, but for smaller beds within a defined landscape, some kind of border improves the appearance and keeps the garden from migrating into the surrounding lawn.

Raised Beds

If soil conditions or topography challenge your success at gardening in dug beds, raise them up. Home gardeners today embrace this planting method for its versatility, production yield, and convenience. By building up soil about 2 feet (61 cm) above ground level—one-third of the bed is existing soil and mixed and stacked on top is one-third peat and one-third compost—you create a welcome soil environment for planting.

Soil quality is one reason for high production yields from raised beds: about 0.6 pounds (0.3 kg) of vegetables per square foot (.09 sq. m), or more. Soil does not suffer compaction from foot traffic or machinery. Vegetables planted at high densities are placed far enough away to avoid crowding, but close enough to shade and choke out weeds. In raised beds, you can better control soil pH. You can water plants easily with soaker hoses, which deliver water to soil and roots rather than spraying leaves and inviting disease.

Raised beds are generally no wider than 4 feet (1.2 m), and you can extend them as long as you please. Position beds at a north-south orientation for low-growing crops so both sides of the bed gain exposure to direct sunlight. Taller crops thrive when positioned east-west. A system of beds can face different directions, depending on what you plant in them. Frames or borders are optional.

Building Raised Beds

Raised beds are convenient homes for vegetables, herbs, and flowers. You can establish the perfect growing environment and maintain healthy soil easily in a raised bed, and these structures are not difficult to build either. Follow these step-by-step instructions to construct one of your own.

PROJECT

TOOLS & MATERIALS

- Basic tools
- Reciprocating saw
- Stakes and string
- 8 ft. 4 × 4 timbers (6)
- 6" galvanized nails
- Roofing nails
- Topsoil
- Plantings
- Mulch
- Wood-sealer protectant

How to Build a Raised Planting Bed

1. Use a shovel to remove the grass inside the outline, then dig a trench for the first row of timbers.

2. Level timbers in the trench, then lay the next layer, staggering the joints. Drill holes and drive nails through the holes.

3. Place the third layer of landscape timbers over the second, staggering the joints. Secure the timbers in place with nails. Drill ½" (1.3 cm) drainage holes through the bottom row of the timbers. Line the bed with landscape fabric.

4. Fill the bed with topsoil, then plant your garden. Apply a 3" (7.6 cm) layer of mulch and water the garden.

Herb Gardens

There's no better way to add spice to your cooking or garnish a family'supper than to include fresh herbs from your garden. If your herbs are within eyeshot of the kitchen window, you can quickly access your garden and snip what you need. Herbs can grow in containers or modest gardens, and they even can be tucked into flower beds if you want to add scent and interest to your landscape. What's more, herbs are great for beginner gardeners: they're fairly low-maintenance, basically pest free, and require little, if any, fertilization.

Some herbs are annuals and require planting each year. Others are biennials that live two seasons and bloom the second season. Perennials bloom each season. Start out with a bed of healthy soil (refer to Tilling & Amending Soil, page 88, for suggestions). Herbs thrive in raised beds.

Traditionally, herb gardens feature symmetrical paths to define the structure of the planting space and a central decorative feature such as a birdbath, statuary, water feature, or ornate planter. Beds are planted in geometric patterns: triangles with a diamond center, square, or circle with sections that look like pie slices.

Common Herb Picks

Basil, *Ocimum basilicum*

Broadleaf English thyme, *Thymus vulgaris*

Narrow-leaf French thyme, *Thymus vulgaris 'Narrow Leaf French'*

Sage, *Salvia*

Chives, *Allium schoenoprasum*

Golde lemon thyme, *Thymus citriodorus*

Oregano, *Origanum vulgare*

Sweet marjoram, *Majorana hortensis*

Rosemary (potted), *Rosmarinus officinalis*

Parsley, *Petroselinum crispum*

Lemon verbena, *Aloysia triphylla*

French tarragon, *Artemisia dracunculus*

Container Gardens

Containers are ideal test sites for flowers and herbs you want to experiment with before including in your garden. Just remember, soil is shallow in containers and it tends to dry out quickly. The good news is you can change the site easily if sunlight is inadequate, and some plant varieties will perform equally well indoors.

A CUTTING GARDEN is a flower garden that is designed to be able to sacrifice some of its blossoms on a regular basis without looking like it has just been overrun by a stampede of buffalo.

Cutting Gardens

If the thought of clipping flowers from your plant beds makes you cringe, start a cutting garden and grow a generous supply that you can use to build beautiful bouquets for your farm home. Choose a variety of annuals and perennials, and include species with staggered bloom times so your garden will flourish from spring through fall. As with other gardens, sunlight and soil are critical success factors. Mind both of these variables as you select flowers to plant.

There are various flower garden styles, and you'll gain inspiration by reading any number of gardening periodicals available on magazine racks today. Cottage gardens are wild with a hodge-podge of plantings and characterized by varieties such as viburnum, hydrangea, English roses, daylily, coreopsis, and foxglove. Cottage gardens contain "rooms" of flowers and always feature living walls (shrubbery), fences, arbors, gates, and pathways. Or, you may wish to simply plant rows of flowers in large beds, much as you would plant a field of corn.

This arrangement works well if you want to grow flowers in bulk to sell or if you want the appearance of a sea of flowers. Regardless of the garden design you choose as you plant your flowery world, remember to start small. You can always add beds, expand your garden, and experiment with new varieties as you gain more experience.

Gardening by the Seasons

Annuals: anise, basil, chervil, coriander, dill, summer savory, rosemary, German chamomile, lemon verbena

Biennials: parsley, caraway

Perennials: chives, bee balm, fennel, mint, Mexican marigold mint, French tarragon, sweet marjoram, broadleaf English thyme, narrow-leaf French thyme, silver edge thyme, golden lemon thyme, sage, oregano

EVEN IN THE SUBURBS, hungry deer have become a major nuisance for both vegetable gardeners and landscapers.

Critter Control

Uninvited guests can destroy a vegetable garden or flower bed. Deer, rabbits, moles, rodents—these are not members of the cast of wildlife characters you want to attract to your property if you plan to harvest a bounty. They're hungry and persistent. You can't stop these foragers completely from feasting on your land, but you can contain them with fencing, repellents, traps, and smart planting strategies.

Deer

Netting and fencing are most effective for keeping deer out of gardens and away from landscape beds. Repellents will work for some time, but deer eventually grow immune to scents and you'll have to switch products. While deer do not have a palate for plants such as echinacea, if they are truly starving, they will munch on just about anything.

Netting will protect young shrubs and seedlings, tubing protects tree trunks, and fences will send the keep-out message to deer that try to enter a garden space. You can purchase electric, conventional 8-foot (2.4 m) fences of woven wire; single-wire electric fences; and mesh barriers. Deer will try to go under or through a fence rather than over it, so opt for double and triple wire fences if your deer population is high.

Homemade Repellent

To repel deer from a problem area, try this kitchen remedy. Mix 80 percent water with 20 percent raw eggs. Pour into a spray bottle and use as a homemade repellent. This formula lasts about 30 days and is weather resistant.

Small Pests

Gophers will snack on roots and plants, while moles prefer insects and worms. Both tunnel and burrow underneath plant beds and gardens to feast on their food of choice. The problem is, the air spaces from their tunnels can damage plant root systems. You can prevent their burrowing by planting in raised beds with sides at least 18 inches (45.7 cm) tall. Line bed bottoms with poultry wire or hardware cloth. Raised beds also discourage jumpers like rabbits.

If you already have a mole problem, methods such as flooding or trapping will chase them from their holes. Gophers are more stubborn. Scare tactics like using dynamite do not work nor do vibrating and ultrasonic devices. Frustrated gardeners have tried everything from road flares to human hair. Trapping, poison, and gasses are the most common techniques for removal. For trapping, use a gopher probe to determine the direction of the tunnel. Dig two holes along the tunnel and position two box traps so their openings face opposite directions. Poison can be purchased as grains or cakes. Gas out gophers by igniting a bit of sulfur, forcing it down the hole, and covering it until smoke engulfs the gopher residence.

Nature's Controls

To avoid fencing, netting, and other eyesores that, while effective, ruin the ambiance of country life, grow natural barriers and keep pets that work as garden lookouts. Prickly foliage such as sedum scares off deer and rabbits. Grow a border of abrasive plants, including globe thistle, cardoon, and berkheya. In general, deer will avoid herbs, though they may be tempted to snack on basil. Other undesirable flowers that deer and rabbits will avoid are daisies, poppies, narcissus, aster, and coreopsis.

Meanwhile, the family dog or cat will discourage pests from invading your beds. Hawks that hunt on your property will swoop down and pick up small mammals. Nocturnal barn owls will tame a gopher population that tends to sneak up from their burrows at night.

A FOUR-LEGGED SECURITY GUARD will help keep rodents and other small animals out of your gardens.

A GOOD FENCE is just about the only way to keep deer out of your garden (but if they're hungry enough, even that won't always stop them).

FRESH PRODUCE FOR ALL SEASONS is one of the great reasons to plant vegetable gardens. From peas in the spring to summer squash to potatoes and garlic in the fall, there is no substitute for homegrown.

Growing Vegetables

A vibrant vegetable garden bursting with colorful produce ensures that your dinner table will never be short of homegrown delicacies. You can cruise by your backyard beds and pick produce as you would in a grocery store, except your bounty is far better. Then there's the personal satisfaction you gain from growing your own—watching seeds peek out from the earth, observing how blossoms evolve into fruit, and how plants grow tall as they reach for the sun. Your garden is a nutritious masterpiece, and it requires careful planning, vegetable selection, partnering of complementary cultivars, and application of all those rules about soil quality and bed design we discussed earlier.

Which Veggies to Grow?

Seed catalogs provide inspiration in cold winter months, when you should begin planning which cultivars you will grow in your garden. Choose reliable guides that provide details on fruit size, flavor, germination, and regional requirements, drought and heat tolerance, and disease resistance. Catalogs feature a greater selection than nurseries, though you can always buy staples at a garden center. As you peruse a catalog, choose a couple of cultivars from each vegetable category. You could start with a pair each of leafy greens, pod vegetables, root crops, plus tomatoes and other personal favorites. Introduce a couple of new vegetables each year and see what thrives in your garden. Take time to learn what growing conditions each prefers and how plants react in your space. Then welcome new vegetables to your garden family.

As you decide what produce to grow, find out if there are any disease problems in your region. Contact a cooperative extension agency and obtain details on disease pressures and common pests so you can choose vegetables wisely. Play it safe by choosing cultivars labeled as disease resistant or disease tolerant if you want to limit the use of pesticides.

Compatibility

Some vegetables get along in a garden like "peas and carrots." You've probably heard this reference before, but its origin is in the science of plant companionship. Yes, some vegetables are natural partners that benefit each other when planted close. On the other hand, some combinations are troublesome, and one plant will inhibit the growth of another. Potatoes inhibit the growth of tomatoes and squash; beans inhibit onions; carrots inhibit dill. You can plant these antagonists together in the same garden, just don't put them side by side.

For Starters

Some easy-to-grow vegetables for your garden include asparagus, beets, bush beans, cabbages, carrots, leaf lettuces, spinach, onions, leeks, peppers, summer squashes, sweet potatoes, and tomatoes.

Vegetable Companions

Asparagus	tomato, parsley, basil
Bean	potato, marigold, cucumber, corn, strawberry, celery
Beet	lettuce, cabbage, onion
Broccoli	potato, celery, dill, beet, onion
Cabbage	oregano, potato, celery, dill, beet, onion
Carrots	pea, lettuce, chive, onion, rosemary, sage, tomato
Celery	leek, tomato, bean, cauliflower, cabbage
Corn	potato, pea, bean, cucumber, squash, pumpkin
Cucumber	bean, corn, pea, radish
Eggplant	bean
Garlic	beet, strawberry, tomato, lettuce, chamomile
Lettuce	carrot, radish, strawberry, cucumber
Melon	pumpkin, corn, radish
Onion	broccoli, beet, carrot, eggplant, strawberry, tomato, lettuce
Pea	potato, carrot, turnip, radish, cucumber, corn, bean
Pepper	basil
Potato	eggplant, bean, corn, cabbage
Pumpkin	corn
Radish	pea, lettuce, cucumber, beet, spinach, melon, tomato, bean
Spinach	strawberry, radish
Tomato	chive, onion, parsley, asparagus, carrot
Turnips	pea, bean
Watermelon	potato

Vegetable Families

Vegetables are grouped in families based on their rooting habits, foliage, and other traits. The top 10 families of vegetable crops grown in home gardens are as follows:

Amaryllidaceae: chive, garlic, leek, onion

Chenopodiaceae: beet, chard, spinach

Cruciferae: broccoli, brussel sprout, cabbage, cauliflower, Chinese cabbage, kale, kohlrabi, mustard greens, radish, rutabaga, turnip

Cucurbitaceae: chayote, cucumber, muskmelon, pumpkin, summer and winter squash, watermelon

Compositae: artichoke, endive, lettuce

Gramineae (Poaceae): corn

Lillaceae: asparagus

Leguminosae: dry bean, fava bean, lima bean, pea, snap bean

Solanaceae: eggplant, pepper, potato, tomato

Umbelliferae: carrot, celery, celedac, Florence fennel, parsley, parsnip

SHOWN HERE: Closeup of the first tomatoes and cucumbers of the season. Also in this organic garden is rosemary and oregano (seen in background).

LEAFY GREENS THRIVE IN LATE SPRING, and many varieties continue to produce throughout the growing season. This consistency makes them well suited to anchor your vegetable garden as more seasonal fruits come and go.

Timing

A well-timed garden will produce a rotation of fresh veggies from spring through fall. Essentially, develop a succession plan for your garden by planting a variety of vegetables with staggered ripening times. Your goal is to never have an unplanted spot in your garden, therefore maximizing your yield. There are a few different ways to plan your garden for a continuous bounty. First, choose a combination of annuals that must be replanted each season, and perennials that overwinter and reemerge each spring. Perennials include asparagus, rhubarb, and artichoke. Most other vegetables are annuals.

Include a variety of cool- and warm-season vegetables. Cool-season cultivars germinate and grow at lower temperatures and are ideal for jump-starting your garden in spring and sustaining your bounty through fall. Some cool-season vegetables are broccoli, cabbage, kale, onion, pea, radish, spinach, turnip, and garlic. The seeds for warm-season crops will rot if planted in cold, damp soil. Summer performers include cantaloupe, cucumber, eggplant, pepper, pumpkin, squash, sweet corn, tomato, and watermelon.

Now, back to the succession plan. There are a few ways to maximize your garden space. First, plant in cool- and warm-season groupings. Once a crop is harvested, replant it with a different crop. Another option is to plant the same crop continuously through the season. The third method is to plant all of your vegetables once in the spring, ensuring that they have varying maturity dates. This requires mixing cool- and warm-season crops, including annuals and perennials, and noting which crops will peak and expire quickly versus those that take all season to mature. This method is the most effective means of establishing a continuous harvest.

Orchards & Berries

A pick-your-own sign posted in front of a family farm can invite quite a bit of traffic during harvest season. You may remember a childhood excursion to pluck fresh apples and pears from orchard trees. Do you recall leaving a strawberry patch with sweet-stained fingers and a sour belly after sampling one too many? With a small amount of acreage, you can have a field day on your own land. In a small backyard, dwarf trees can be trained into an espalier form, flattened against a wall or fence. You don't need too much surface area to grow blueberries. As with raising any crop, growing fruit successfully requires sufficient knowledge to provide optimal growing conditions.

Fruit Trees

A few semi-dwarf apple trees can produce up to 12 bushels of crisp fruit—same goes for pears. There's no need to dedicate an entire acre to fruit trees if you only want to grow enough to feed your family. Select from various sizes of apple and pear trees: standard, semi-dwarf, and dwarf. Standard trees take a few years to develop before bearing fruit, while dwarf trees produce faster but fewer apples. Your decision will depend on yield expectations and your equipment. Aside from these staples, you may experiment with apricots, sour cherries, figs, plums, peaches, nectarines, persimmons, walnuts, almonds, and hazelnuts.

As you plan your orchard, consider ripening times for different species. For example, apricots and cherries ripen earlier in the season, while pears peak later along with apples. If your goal is to pick fresh fruit all summer and fall, choose trees with staggered ripening periods. But remember, your region may not accommodate a variety of trees; you're limited to what Mother Nature will nurture on your land.

As you plan your fruit orchard, think about what you will do with the bounty. A few fruit trees may produce enough for your family to enjoy, and for you to can or gift to neighbors. But perhaps your goals are loftier and you want to invite the public to your property to pick fruit. Picking farms are appealing to families who want to expose their children to country life and enjoy a Sunday afternoon activity. In such a case, you will plant a more generous orchard, allowing for the fact that a couple of trees may not produce heartily because of unforeseen conditions (pests, disease, etc.).

A SPECIAL TOOL FOR REACHING APPLES on high branches helps this grower collect the bounty.

Do not be tempted to plant an orchard right on top of your vegetable garden. You will need to spray fruit trees with pesticides, and this treatment could harm the produce. Meanwhile, your garden can host harmful nematodes that invade soil and damage trees. Dedicate separate areas for your fruits and veggies so you can tend to their individual needs.

AN APPLE TREE can take 15 to 20 years before it reaches full production.

Site Selection

Before deciding which type of fruit or nut trees to plant, talk to your neighbors. Are there other orchards in the area? What species succeed in your region? Fruit trees require time to chill, a period when temperatures drop below 45 degrees Fahrenheit (7 degrees Celsius). This varies by species. If winter is too mild or overly harsh, the harvest will suffer. Generally, fruit trees prefer regions where temperatures seldom drop below −4 degrees Fahrenheit (−20 degrees Celsius). There is some wiggle room, but expect a poor season if your thermometer dips below −13 degrees Fahrenheit (−25 degrees Celsius) for an extensive period. Every region has its downside. The Great Plains states are too cold and dry. Northern states weather tough winters. Southern regions may not provide trees with the necessary winter chill to produce a healthy crop. Of course, all of these regions contain successful orchards, and your micro-climate is an equal player in whether fruit trees will thrive.

Your micro-climate is your land: the topography, soil content, and sun exposure. As you select a site for an orchard, examine the soil and choose a well-drained area. Sandy loam soil is ideal. Also, keep in mind that areas near water, such as a lake, tend to offer more temperate conditions.

Tree Pollination

Trees produce by self- and cross-pollination, depending on the species. Cross-pollinating species need a "mate" of a different variety. Apples and pears cross pollinate, as do plums, sweet cherries, almonds, and hazelnuts. When planting, a rule of thumb is to place a pollenizer for every three main variety trees. In larger orchards, you may integrate pollenizers by planting a couple rows of these mates for every four rows of the main variety. The point is to expose each main variety tree to the pollenizer so your orchard will maximize its fruit-bearing potential.

Self-pollinating trees include apricot, sour cherry, fig, peach, nectarine, persimmon, and walnut. Plant one variety of each of these species with no worry about fertility.

BERRIES TASTE BEST when they are picked fresh. Plant a variety of species so you can feed on fresh berries throughout spring and summer.

Berries

Berry crops demand the labor of picking, but if you can recruit your family to help, you'll enjoy fresh fruit, jams, juices, and pies all year round. There's nothing better than the tart taste of fresh-grown blueberries buried in homemade muffins. After tasting these gems, you won't want to resort to overplumped grocery store berries that are bred mostly to avoid damage in transport.

Strawberries, blackberries, and raspberries require soil with a pH of 5.5 to 7.0, while blueberries prefer acidic soils with a pH between 4.0 and 5.5. They all need well-drained soil but plenty of water to feed their growth. Irrigate your berries during dry summer times to preserve your harvest. Following are additional berry particulars:

Blueberries: These woody perennials take three to four years to grow to mature size. Prune them to a height of 5 to 8 feet (1.5 to 2.4 m) and a width of 3 to 8 feet (0.9 to 2.4 m). Blueberries struggle when winter temperatures drop below −20 degrees Fahrenheit (-29 degrees Celsius) and when the growing season is less than 160 days; they require a chill period (temperatures under 45 degrees Fahrenheit [7 degrees Celsius]) of at least 1,000 hours.

Blackberries and Raspberries (Brambles): Woody and thorny, their roots live for years in brambles, and stems usually live for two seasons. They vegetate in the first year and bear fruit in the spring of the second season. However, raspberries fruit in the fall on first-year canes and the next spring on the same canes. They tolerate most well-drained soil types. Raspberries thrive in areas with cold winters, withstanding temperatures as low as −35 degrees Fahrenheit (-37 degrees Celsius), depending on the variety. They struggle in regions where winter weather fluctuates. Blackberries cannot tolerate temperatures lower than −15 degrees Fahrenheit (-26 degrees Celsius), and the thornless varieties prefer winters that do not drop below 0 (-17 degrees Celsius).

Strawberries: These perennial herbaceous plants grow runners and hug the soil, making them susceptible to disease. They are available in a range of cultivars suited for various climates, so you are likely to find some type of strawberry that will thrive on your land. The key is to plant them in well-drained soil, control weeds, and water regularly during the growing season.

RAISING CROPS FOR ANIMAL FOOD prevents erosion on your land and reduces the amount you must spend on straw and other feed.

Forage Crops

If you raise animals, you may also want to raise crops to feed them. Forage crops can fill acres of land with pasture, hay fields, straw, and other feed for your hobby farm pets. Even if you don't keep animals, you can seed several acres for hay rather than mow or bush hog the area. You don't need a herd of cattle to justify hay production. Grow just enough for a bunny or lamb, if you choose. In any case, forage crops are great for beginners because they are relatively low in maintenance needs and pastureland does not need to be tilled regularly.

Pasture

Animals love a grassy area to exercise and find snacks. Your pasture can cater to both of these needs and even supply nutritional value, depending on what type of forage crops you plant. Generally speaking, pasture is comprised of grasses, legumes, and broadleaf plants. Forage crop selection depends on the land's soil temperature and topography. Cool-season grasses prefer well-drained soil and include bromegrass and orchard grass (known for shade tolerance). Warm-season grasses perform best in heavy fertile lowland soils and include bluegrass, tall fescue, ryegrass, timothy, and Reed canarygrass. You'll likely grow a combination of grasses and legumes, mixing in clover, alfalfa, vetch, or birdsfoot trefoil to provide a healthy mix for your animals. A county extension agent will best advise you on practical pasture grasses to suit your animals and land.

Hay

Hay is a staple winter meal for animals, and you can grow your own if you have the manpower, equipment (utility tractor with baler), and desire to work the land. Purchase hay from a supplier, or you can grow it and pay a custom baler to manage the harvest process for an hourly or per-bale fee. Hay falls into the following categories: grass, legume, mixed, and cereal grain straw.

You may be surprised to learn that hay for horses isn't palatable for sheep. Grow (or buy) hay that contains appropriate leaf nutrition for the animals you raise. Horses like hay from grass, alfalfa, and other legumes. Mature goats prefer a grass-legume mix, while their kids enjoy alfalfa, clover, vetch, or soybean hay. Sheep also lean toward leafy rather than course hay. Alpacas and llamas like orchard grass hay.

Hay must be kept dry, otherwise it will mold and may contain toxins that are harmful to animals. The best bet is to store hay indoors in a barn or outbuilding, such as a shed—and do not store wet hay. It can spontaneously combust when chemicals within the wet stack produce a dangerous heating reaction. If you can't spare room in a covered area, set hay bales on pallets and cover with tarps. Build the top-center row of hay higher to create a tenting effect so water will run off the tarp surface.

STORE HAY in an area free of moisture, such as in a barn loft.

FARMERS' MARKETS provide an outlet for commercial farmers and hobbyists alike.

Preserving the Bounty

After a successful growing season, you may harvest more than you can consume—or store, or give away to neighbors. The good news is that your bounty is thanks to attention to your crops and the soil, water, sunlight, and nutrients they need to thrive. The problem may be what to do with all the extra produce. This is a good problem to have if you want to start a roadside vegetable stand, sell your produce at farmers' markets, or make preserves so you can taste the summer and fall throughout the winter months.

Consumers today are more interested in where their food comes from and how it is grown. If you can market your produce as organic, abiding by standards set by the USDA's National Organic Program, you will earn the business of those conscious customers. But even if you're too small a producer to qualify for official designations, don't underestimate the power of local appeal.

CREATING DRIED FLORAL ARRANGEMENTS and potpourri are good ways to extend short growing seasons so you can enjoy the bounty of your farmstead all year round.

WELCOME PASSERS BY TO YOUR LAND and your bounty by setting up a roadside vegetable stand.

AFTER PRESERVING fruits into jam and herbs into savory pestos, an ambitious gardener can enjoy gifts from the garden year-round.

LAVENDER IS A USEFUL, aromatic herb that can provide a bounty to make scented candles and other household luxuries, such as bubble baths and fancy soaps.

CHAPTER 5

Raising Animals

On most farms and hobby farms, animals are just as much a part of the landscape as a prized flower garden, an orchard of fruit-bearing trees, or a quaint farmhouse with a gravel road. Plus, animals are lively, lovable creatures that often become cherished family pets. Of course, there are reasons for raising farm animals that are less warm-and-fuzzy than cultivating pets. Feeding your family farm-fresh eggs, unpasteurized milk, and naturally raised meat that actually has flavor are also great incentives to add some livestock to your farm.

Your Animal Kingdom

A hobby farm without animals seems naked, stark, a bit ho-hum. What's country life without the heaping dose of personality that a clutch of curious chickens, playful pigs, and lovable sheep bring to a farm? Talk about free entertainment! Goats are class clowns with their antics, and skittish sheep run in wooly packs across pastures as a guard llama keeps an eye out for predators. Trusty horses become your best friends—all of the animals do, really. Hobby farm pets earn as much attention as a spoiled hound dog, except livestock can't curl up in bed with you at night. Even with a couple of acres of land, you can cast your own crew of farm characters, which will depend on you for food, shelter, and care.

Livestock and Responsibility

Animals are a real commitment. You can't haul them to a kennel and jet off for a week-long vacation, though you may be lucky enough to find a dependable farm sitter willing to manage your chores. On a day-to-day basis, raising animals means never-ending chores, such as cleaning stalls, mending fences, scraping muck from dirty hooves, feeding, and cleaning up manure. You will worry when one of your animals is not healthy. Your animals will interfere with dinner plans, weekend excursions, and just about any other activity you schedule that doesn't include them. Animals are needy, after all, but they can't help it. You can't press pause if your sheep goes into labor at 3 a.m., and your animals may need their breakfast before you get to have yours.

If this sounds dramatic, well, it is. But when you're ready to be an animal parent, none of these things will matter. You will camp out in the barn all night waiting for a lamb to be born, and you will forgive a conniving goat that breaks through fencing and tramples over your car, leaving hoof-sized dents in its path. Understand, farm animals will change your life—usually for the better.

ANIMALS ARE WONDERFUL TEACHERS for children, who can learn responsibility by caring for them and gain companionship from loyal farm "pets."

ALL FARM ANIMALS require extensive care and attention, so be certain that you are prepared to make some sacrifices before you commit to obtaining livestock for your farm.

Farm Sitters

If you are fortunate to live next to helpful neighbors who have experience in the type of animals you raise, get to know them. Bring them wine or chocolate. (It can't hurt.) They will be a valuable resource for you as you learn how to care for animals on your farm. They may even agree to feed and watch over your livestock if you must leave for a night. You'll probably need to seek out a professional farm sitter if you plan to leave your land for a week or longer.

Whether you turn the reins over to a neighbor, friend, or professional, be sure to leave them written directions. It's a good idea to keep a notebook with "chapters" for each of your animals. Reserve a section for your chickens, sheep, horses, etc. In each chapter, write down the animals' feeding requirements; make notes about past illnesses and immunizations. This record will not only serve as a valuable document for your veterinarian, it will provide anyone who cares for your farm in your absence the vital stats they need.

BUILD A SAFE, SECURE HOME for animals before welcoming them to your farm.

Animal Infrastructure

Before you bring home a boxful of day-old chicks from the feed store or introduce a few sheep to your backyard, prepare your property for their arrival. Think of it as building a nest. Consider where animals will sleep, what they will eat, and where they will roam and play. Build fencing and shelter, provide a water source and feed, and find a dependable veterinarian who can administer immunizations and teach you the basics of animal husbandry. You'll also need patience, but that's a whole different story. So if you're perusing the bill for a livestock auction or a neighbor has tempted you with an offer to purchase a pig, be sure to work out all the details before you agree.

Room for Roamers

The first order of business is to determine whether your land is zoned for the type of animals you want to raise. Depending on the location of your property, your county may set limits on the distance your pigpen must be away from your property line, for example. Pigs, especially, can offend neighbors who don't want to wake up and smell the sty. There may also be requirements for grazing animals such as cows, and you may need to obtain licenses and owner/breeder permits from federal, state, and local authorities.

What animals will your land accommodate? A couple of acres will suit horses, sheep, chickens, a couple of goats, rabbits, pigs—any of these animals in moderation. Animals need room to poke around, to play, to live freely. They should not be raised in a situation where they compete fiercely for pasture food. Housing too many animals in a grazing area is an unfair way to feed animals.

Shelter

A barn is not necessary for every species, though most animals require some type of shelter for protection from the elements and, perhaps, for sleeping. The type of roof you put over animals' heads depends largely on where you live. If your property is in Minnesota, animals will require a more sturdy, draft-resistant abode than if your land is located in New Mexico. In southern regions, keeping animals cool is a concern, and the shelter will require plenty of ventilation and, probably, fans to circulate breezes.

Following are some basic shelter guidelines for common farm animals:

Pigs: A crude structure will suffice, as long as it is free of drafts. Pigs prefer not to sleep and eat in the same area, so divide a pen and dedicate one space for the trough and waterer and another straw-lined space for sleeping. Generally speaking, hog houses should be no closer than 500 feet (152.5 m) away from your neighbors' properties.

Chickens: Chicks need heat, light, and protection from predators. Mature chickens live in coops or a laying house. Even if you allow chicks to run free-range, they should sleep in a coop that can be secured at night to prevent predators, such as coyotes, from entering.

Horses: You'll need a well-constructed barn for your horses, with straw-lined stalls that allow enough room for them to move freely. Your barn may include a breezeway or center aisle so you can easily access each stall. A loft area can hold hay, feed, and other supplies.

Sheep: A barn or shed with plenty of ventilation will work for sheep. Depending on the climate, you may keep them in a hoop house, which is a greenhouse structure with an arched metal frame covered with heavy fabric.

Goats: Protect goats from wet and cold with a three-sided barn or a shed with a straw bed.

Rabbits: In mild climates, hutches can be placed outdoors in a shaded area. In cold climates, keep hutches in a shelter that will protect them from wind and cold. A space heater will help maintain a 40-degree Fahrenheit (4.4-degree Celsius) temperature in the space.

Pigs　　　　**Chickens**

Horses　　　　**Sheep**

Goats　　　　**Rabbits**

Animal Trailers

How will your horses, pigs, sheep, and other barnyard pals get from point A to point B? Investigate trailer options as you consider the tools you'll need to care for animals.

PLAN MOBILE ACCOMMODATIONS for animals such as horses, which require special trailers, equipment, and tack for safe transportation.

A GOOD, STRONG FENCE IS THE BEST INSURANCE you can obtain for goats, hogs, and other animals with a strong sense of wanderlust.

Fencing

The animals you keep will dictate what kind of fencing you should build on your land. Goats are especially tricky and will gnaw and break through fencing. Your best bet is a woven-wire fence with posts of steel or wood, with added protection from two strands of barbed wire, one at the top and one at the bottom of the fence. Pigs like to outsmart fencing systems, hence the phrase "hog-tight fence." Build a fence of woven wire or permanent wood,

at least 3 feet (0.9 m) tall. We discuss specific fencing needs for each species in the following chapters.

As you consider fencing materials, also determine whether you will need to create paddocks to accomplish managed intensive grazing (MIG). This is a rotational system of grazing, whereby pasture is divided into smaller areas. Animals are moved from one zone to the next after a number of days, which preserves the integrity of the pastures.

Other Resources

Aside from shelter and fencing, provide animals with feed, pastures for grazing (in some cases), and clean water. Your job is made easier with customized waterers and feeders available on the market, and if you have money to burn, there are plenty of bells and whistles for your barn. Raising animals is a serious investment—and much of the expense will come without notice. You'll open your wallet when animals fall sick, a predator wipes out your herd, or you must build a new shelter or repair fencing. Before you bring home a barnyard of friends, be sure you have resources set aside to care for them in dire emergencies.

AUTOMATIC WATER AND FEED DEVICES allow cows, horses, and sheep to quench their thirst and satisfy an appetite without your help.

THIS LARGE WATER TROUGH is a portable solution. More than one horse could easily nose in to get a drink here.

Starting Out

So have you made the big decision? Will it be chickens, pigs, a couple of horses, a flock of sheep—or the whole kit and caboodle?

If your animal experience is limited to walking your dog or emptying a cat litter box, start small with your farm venture and begin with basics. Chickens are an excellent indoctrination to the world of barnyard pets. They require little space, are easy to care for, and provide the reward of fresh eggs, which are far better than what you buy in the store.

As you obtain additional animals, be sure to choose species that best fit your land, temperament, experience, and time allowance. If you're timid, wait until you grow more confident with your handling skills before adopting flighty sheep or a goat that will try to outsmart you.

Compatibility counts and with that comes control. But also know that your care and affection plays a key role in this. Animals need and deserve your attention, and in return they will be cooperative, even if sometimes stubborn.

Also important is to select animals that will be comfortable on your property. How hot or cold is the region where you live? While you can make accommodations in the type of shelter you provide animals, your farm pets will be much happier if they aren't shivering through the winter or sweating out the summer heat. Some extreme climates simply do not cater to every animal.

A GOAT OWNER EXAMINES eyes and teeth. Before you purchase an animal, enlist a veterinarian or an experienced animal owner to ensure the new "baby" you will bring home is healthy.

THESE HOLSTEIN COWS are being sold at auction.

Obtaining Livestock

You can purchase animals at auction, through a broker, or from another owner, in which case you will enter what is known as a treaty deal. You may also seek out an animal rescue organization, such as Farm Sanctuary (www.farmsanctuary.com), which operates coast-to-coast shelters for rescue, rehabilitation, and lifelong care for animals that have been subjected to cruelty and neglect. There are pros and cons to each of these animal acquisition methods. If you're new at all this, you may find it easiest to go the treaty deal route and buy an animal from a private party.

When you call on an owner with a desired animal for sale, it's not a bad idea to show up a little early—before the farmer expects you. This may not conform with high-society manners, but one of the goals of your visit is to observe how animals behave in their environment and how they interact with their barn mates. If a horse is buck wild when you pull up to the owner's gate 15 minutes early, you can probably bet the owner planned to settle him down before your arrival. If you are a first-time animal owner or inexperienced with the species

you are about to buy, ask an educated friend or neighbor to accompany you and offer opinions. Inquire about immunizations, breeding records (for show animals), and for major purchases hire a veterinarian to perform a general checkup on the animal in question. Before you arrive to visit the animal, you should have done your homework on the species, gaining an understanding of its food, shelter, and land needs.

Your Best Vet

Before you purchase an animal, contact local veterinarians and find out whether they qualify to treat the species you plan to buy. If you cannot find a vet in your area who will treat the llama you want so badly, find out how far you'll have to drive to reach someone who will. Remember, sickness, births, and other animal events never happen at convenient times. If you must drive, think through the logistics of how you will transport your animal and the time it will take to reach the vet.

Breeding Basics

Breeding is no business for the faint of heart. In fact, you may be a dyed-in-the-wool animal lover with a barn full of creatures you care for and still have difficulty with the emotional aspects of breeding livestock. But if you are of a mind to make your farm a true working farm, breeding is one area you should venture into.

There are a couple of reasons to breed: to increase the size of a sheep flock, cow herd, or chicken clutch; or to produce animals to sell for profit. While birthing is next to impossible to avoid anytime you have male and female animals cohabiting, breeding is a deliberate exercise that requires knowledge and planning—at least on the farmer's part.

For those who produce show animals, the breeding process is actually quite scientific. A breeder will keep careful records and mate certain males and females to produce a desired coat color or to ensure that an attractive physical characteristic is passed down through the line. Breeding can be a full-time job. Most hobby farmers gradually polish their skills at managing the birthing process, but they usually stop short of delving into serious breeding unless they have plenty of free time. If you are not interested in offspring from your animals, have a vet spay or neuter them.

BABY EWES DRINK from a bottle after they are weaned from their mother sheep.

Ask your vet to be present at birthing time if you are new to the process. He or she can stand by and assist. If a problem develops during birth and a vet is not there, it is often too late to call in help.

Learn about Labor

You can learn a lot about the birthing process from an experienced breeder. Even if you do not plan to breed animals, it is a good idea to prepare yourself for unplanned events by getting to know an expert you can call on for help. He or she can serve as a valuable resource. In the meantime, spend time reading up on birthing risks, problems, and hints to help you ease the process. Ask your vet to recommend books, periodicals, and online resources specific to your animal species.

EVEN IF YOU NEVER PLANNED TO BREED FARM ANIMALS, raising livestock always carries with it the possibility that your animals will reproduce without your approval. Consequently, any animal owner is advised to learn some basic instructions for managing the birthing process.

GESTATION PERIOD CHART
Average gestation period for common farm animals.

Animal	Gestation	Avg. Litter Size
Sheep	148 days	1 or 2
Goats	150 days	1 to 3 (twins are common)
Horses	335 to 340 days	1
Cows	283 days	1
Chickens	22 days	12
Pigs	115 days	8 to 12
Rabbits	31 days	6
Alpaca	335 days	1
Llamas	350 days	1

WHEN PREPARING FOR A NEW ADDITION to your family farm, discuss the specific housing requirements for the baby with your vet—including stable size and location, bedding type, feed, water dishes, sand, heat, and lighting.

WHILE CHICKENS ARE AMONG the easier barnyard animals to raise, they can be loud, at times and they leave a messy trail. But you'll understand why so many hobby farmers keep hens as soon as you taste your first farm-fresh egg.

Chickens

For many reasons, chickens are an ideal introduction to the farm animal kingdom. They're happy-go-lucky and curious—a pleasure to watch—and they live comfortably on land of all types, from roomy ranches to small backyards. If your property is the latter, just be sure your coop isn't too close to the neighbors, who may not appreciate all the cheeping.

In terms of increasing self-sufficiency on the land, chickens provide a two-for-one special: free-range meat and farm-fresh eggs. You may even intend to sell eggs at local farmers' market or post a sign on your mailbox so neighbors and friends can enjoy the bounty. But many property owners simply choose to raise chickens

because poultry is fairly easy to maintain, and chickens seem to go hand in hand with the lifestyle. Have land, raise chickens.

Chickens have distinct personalities. Laying habits, temperaments, and barnyard demeanor depend on the breed of chicken. Similarly, chickens range in size and purpose. You wouldn't raise a layer if you planned to produce meat, in which case you probably wouldn't choose a smaller bantam chicken that only weighs a couple of pounds. Ornamental chickens are a chicken fancier's choice and are bred to show, while meat breeds range in size from broilers to roasters and will feed a family.

So, why do you want chickens?

Perhaps you dream of eggs with thick, sturdy sunshine yolks that are unbeatable for baking (and perhaps for selling at a farmers' market stand). Maybe you want to dress the dinner table with a fresh bird. Not sure? If you want both eggs and meat, you're safe with a dual-purpose breed such as the barred Plymouth Rock.

Next, consider the size flock you will need to fulfill your goals. This depends on land availability and how much produce you wish to gain. In other words, if volume of eggs or meat matters, then you increase your "production line." Generally, two hens produce an egg a day for each person in a family of four. If your reason for raising chickens is to enjoy the company of a low-maintenance feathered pet—the meat and eggs are just a bonus—then a flock of three hens and a rooster will get you started.

Layers

While all chickens produce eggs, laying breeds are more efficient at the job than other breeds; in short, layers lay more eggs. You can expect about 250 eggs per year or more if your layer is more ambitious than most. Laying hens tend to be high-strung, however, and while they lay many eggs, they show little interest in raising chicks.

You may reconsider laying breeds if you want your hens to raise the next generation. Layers simply aren't interested—but they'll keep seconds coming to the breakfast table.

Meat Breeds

These chickens are classified based on size when butchered. Game hens weigh 1 to 3 pounds (.5 to 1.4 kg), broilers (also called fryers) range from 4 to 5 pounds (1.8 to 2.3 kg), and roasters are usually 7 pounds (3.2 kg) or slightly more. You'll find cross-breeds ideal for the backyard, including broiler-roaster hybrids like the Cornish hen or the New Hampshire.

Dual-Purpose Breeds

Larger than layers but more productive (in the egg department) than meat breeds, dual-purpose breeds are the happy medium. Hens will sit on eggs until they hatch, so you can raise the next generation. There are many chickens that fall into this variety, and their temperaments vary. Many dual-purpose breeds are also heritage breeds, meaning they are no longer bred in mass for industry. They like to forage for worms and bugs, are known for disease resistance, and, essentially, are the endangered species of the chicken world.

A CHICKEN COOP is a productive place. On average, a laying hen will yield approximately 250 eggs per year.

Ornamental Chickens

Silky soft plumes, fancy feather-dos, distinct red combs that look like rooster Mohawks—ornamental chickens are bred for looks. Chicken fanciers who raise poultry for pageantry rather than production focus intently on physical characteristics, from body shape to feather pattern. The American Poultry Association sets standards by which show chickens are judged, and fanciers hope to earn the max on a 100-point scale.

Bantams

Bantams are generally half the size of other chicken varieties. A true bantam is not a stunted version of another type. Many chicken varieties have a bantam counterpart, and these are instead referred to as miniatures. Bantams fly about, and they generally have nice temperaments. They produce smaller eggs and really aren't ideal for meat since they weigh just a couple of pounds. Bantam owners love their breed because of their varied colors and feather patterns, petite size, and calm personalities. Bantam roosters, on the other hand, are rather aggressive and cocky, which can be amusing given their diminished stature.

ORNAMENTAL CHICKENS often make good pets. They enjoy human companionship. And they are a fun and visual addition to the yard!

Free Range

The one trait chickens share is their love for pecking around the yard. They are outdoor birds and prefer to roam within limits. They are natural pest controllers, feasting on pests like Japanese beetles, worms, and bugs. Their meat far surpasses feed-raised chicken meat in flavor.

FREE-RANGE CHICKENS like this clucker get plenty of exercise, but they risk being captured by wolves and other predators.

THIS ENCLOSED HEN HOUSE and roaming area provides a safe zone for chickens and turkeys to play outside the coop.

Getting Started

There are several ways you can choose from to make your initial foray into raising chickens. To raise broiler chickens for meat, you can purchase fertilized but unhatched eggs, or you can buy boxfuls of day-old chicks. Broilers grow and mature much more quickly than laying hens. To establish a flock of laying hens, you can buy pullets, which are juvenile hens that are at least 20 weeks old and have begun to lay eggs. You can think of pullets as adolescents, still in need of careful rearing, but not as fragile as chicks or as susceptible to disease. Consider your time before you decide to start a flock. Finding a mature hen to start your flock may be more challenging, as many landowners will not want to sacrifice an established commodity. But this is also an option to consider if you want to skip the brooding step, which requires a special coop and lights.

DAY-OLD CHICKS are sold at hatcheries and feed stores to be raised on farms primarily for meat. Raising them to broiler weight of 4 to 5 lbs. (1.8 to 2.3 kg) usually takes six to eight weeks.

JUVENILE CHICKENS are usually obtained to be put into service as laying hens, not for their meat. Meat species grow much more quickly.

Chick or Pullet?

Chicks are day-old babies, just hatched and in need of careful brooding with heat lamps. Essentially, you must recreate the hen's nest, keeping the chicks warm, dry, and safe from predators (the list of predators should include your family dogs and cats, which typically are very curious about the fuzzy peeps you bring into the barn). Order baby chicks from a hatchery that will ship overnight or purchase them from a farm or feed supply store. Purchasing day-old chicks is more practical than starting with unhatched eggs that will require an incubation facility. Pullets are easiest to manage.

Purchase starter pullets at 24 weeks of age. By then they are vaccinated, and you can worry less about disease in the coop. Pullets do not require a brood environment, which you must create until chicks are old enough to be kept in a coop or laying house. You still must monitor light exposure and heat for growing pullets.

Hens eat about ¼ lb. (.1 kg) of feed per day, and you'll need about 19 lbs. (8.5 kg) of feed to grow a chick to 20 weeks.

A BROODER PEN for a handful of chicks can be made from cardboard and newspaper (for bedding) with a heat lamp to keep the chicks warm.

Food, Shelter & Light

When raising chicks, summer or spring is the best time to start a brood, mainly because temperatures are more favorable. Chicks need heat, light, and protection from predators. So before the arrival of your day-old chicks or pullets, prepare their new home.

A brooder pen should be circular so chicks don't pile up in a corner, and you should allow for about 1 sq. foot (0.09 sq. m) per chick. Think of the brooding pen as an extra large nest with the same environment a mother hen would provide her chicks: warmth and protection from predators, drafts, and water. You can construct your own pen by taping together corrugated cardboard pieces that are approximately 12 inches (30.5 cm) and forming a circle shape. A shallow stock-watering tank will also suffice. A pen should be kept indoors in a barn area or someplace protected from the elements and predators. If you plan to brood a large number of chicks, you may need to build a heatable brooding house. An 8 × 8-foot house (2.4 × 2.4 meters) is large enough for about 50 chicks.

Line the pen with newspaper for the first couple of weeks, which you can easily change once soiled. You may use absorbent litter, such as wood shavings, sawdust, peanut hulls, and ground corncobs. If you use straw, be sure to chop it into fine bits.

Light stimulates maturity and egg production. You should never increase light on a growing pullet or decrease light on a laying hen. (Light hits the retina, sparking the release of eggs.)

Temerature is critical to start chicks. Maintain a 95 degrees Fahrenheit (35 degrees Celsius) temperature in the brooding pen the first week. Lower the temperature by 5 degrees each week until the environment is 70 degrees Fahrenheit (21 degrees Celsius).

There are several types of lamps you can purchase, including infrared lights or battery-operated brooders. If chicks huddle close to the heat source, increase the brooder temperature.

Chicks graduate to a coop or laying house once they are older. Laying pullets start producing eggs gradually when they are 20 to 24 weeks old. They usually hit their peak at 30 weeks.

Collecting Eggs

Collecting eggs from a brooding hen requires a careful hand and sound timing. Expect a good pecking if you reach into the nest while mother is awake. The best time to gently remove eggs from the nest is in the morning or during the night, when hens roost. This is also the best time to pick up a hen and move her, because she won't argue while she's sleeping. And unfortunately, this makes hens easy targets to predators, who can sneak into a coop. Be sure the gate is always secure.

Gather eggs twice a day, more often during temperature extremes when eggs are vulnerable. The longer they sit in the nest, the more likely they are to suffer shell damage. If dirty, dry-clean the eggs or wash them with a special compound you can purchase at farm and feed stores. Wash water should be 100 to 120 degrees Fahrenheit (38 to 49 degrees Celsius). Do not wash them in cold water. Place clean, dry eggs in a carton and refrigerate.

Slaughtering Chickens

Most hobby farmers who raise chickens for meat purchase a number of chicks at once and then raise them until the majority reach a good weight for slaughter (usually 4 to 5 pounds [1.8 to 2.3 kg]—the rapid growth slows quickly after this point). Then, the brood is cleaned, packaged, and usually frozen all at once for maximum efficiency. State regulations vary whether or not a small producer may slaughter and sell animals. In some areas, they must be sent to a licensed and regulated processing center (this tends not to be cost-effective for chickens).

Q&A

Q: What's the difference between a brown egg and a white egg?

A: The difference is merely color. Brown and white eggs contain equal nutritional value. Some hens even lay eggs that are light blue or speckled. No matter the appearance of the shell, what's inside will taste the same.

THIS CHICKEN NESTLES IN HER HEN BOX, watching over eggs. The best time to collect eggs is when the hen is asleep. The hen pictured here likely would not let go of her clutch without pecking at your hand.

PIGLETS cozy up to their mother for feeding.

Pigs

Pigs are personable and intelligent. To watch a pair of porkers waddling in the mud or running about, happy-go-lucky in their pen, is pure entertainment. No wonder good-natured pigs are favorite animals for many landowners. Also, they offer a well-rounded learning experience: lessons on the importance of proper feed mix, daily pigpen cleaning to prevent disease (and smell!), and good old-fashioned recycling. Their composted byproduct is rich fertilizer for soil.

If you have children, raising prize pigs is a popular 4-H project. Besides, pigs enjoy the company of children, who will dote over them. Swine love the spotlight.

At one time, farmers called their pigs "mortgage lifters" because of their profitability when sold at market. This isn't so much the case today, as industrial pork factories squeeze family farm operations out of the market. But for landowners who wish to expand their sustainability beyond the chicken coop, hogs processed at a local livestock slaughtering facility will provide ham, roasts, chops, bacon, and sausage. Whether this is your goal or you simply want to raise pigs for enjoyment, you can start a pigpen with minimal resources.

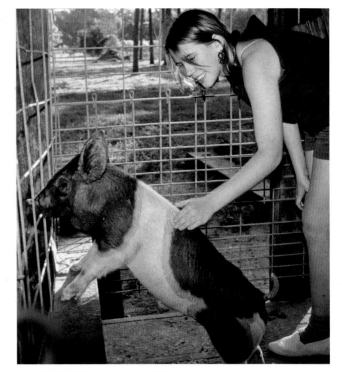

A CURIOUS PIG looks beyond his pen.

Clean the pigpen daily. An ideal time is during a feeding so you can clean out manure and soiled hay and hose out the sleeping area while the pigs are occupied.

Getting Started

Pigs don't require a great deal of land, but they do need a dry, draft-free shelter to protect them from the elements. Be sure to prepare this space before bringing home a sow or gilt (a young female that hasn't bore young). The essentials include:

Hog-tight fence: Contain the feeding area and shelter with a secure fence of woven wire or permanent board. The fence should be about 3 feet (0.9 m) tall.

Shelter: Dedicate a portion of an existing building, such as a barn for a shelter, or construct a simple outbuilding. Ideally, floors should be concrete and sloped for optimum drainage during daily hose-outs. Though a dirt floor works just fine as long as you replace hay bedding daily.

Feed area: Create a separate sleeping and feeding area. A 5 × 5-foot (1.5 × 1.5 meter) sleeping area will accommodate a couple of pigs. The feed area should be twice this size and contain the feed trough, a watering system, and a hose connection. This serves the dual purpose of instant water refills for thirsty pigs—a sow suckling a litter drinks up to 5 gallons a day—and accessibility to your No. 1 pigpen cleaning tool.

Feeder: If you use a trough, be sure there is enough room for all pigs to feed at once. Self-feeders allow pigs to gain weight more quickly, which is ideal if you plan to raise them for market.

Water trough: Keep this full with fresh water at all times.

HUNGRY PIGS dive into their dinner.

Pig Picks

You can purchase weaned pigs from a breeder, at auction, or through classified ads. Find several breeders and compare their facilities. Are they clean? How do the animals look? Are they active with curious eyes and tightly curled tails? Ask for a history of the animals, and inquire about immunizations. The breeder should have all of this information on hand.

Before you choose a pig, learn about different breeds and their behaviors. The eight major hog breeds in the United States include five dark and three white. Dark breeds are known as strong sires that pass their durability and meatiness to offspring. Light breeds are typically doting mothers with exceptional reproductive capabilities. Crossbred sows tend to farrow (give birth) more piglets than purebreds, making them a desirable choice. While you're researching, contact your county agricultural agent and inquire about local regulations regarding the keeping of animals.

If you want to know what a piglet will probably look like when it grows older, look at the sow. Like humans, pigs also tend to develop similar body structure and composition as their parents. If you plan to purchase a pig, you'll want to consider these two qualities: body composition and structure. Take a look at the pig's muscle and "finish." When you look at the rear view of the pig, the muscles in the ham region should be long and thick. The thickest point should be through the stifle, or interior leg. The hind legs should be spread far apart, which also indicates fine ham muscles. Finish is the amount of fat over the muscles of a mature pig, which usually amounts to 125 to 250 pounds. The weight of the pig will depend on the breed (see chart on the right). To evaluate a pig's structure, look at feet, legs, body cavity, and topline. A healthy pig has a deep body cavity and is long and wide.

Common Breeds

Dark Breeds:

Berkshire: black with six white points (nose, tail, and legs); erect ears and a short, dished snout; prefer enclosed facilities; noted for siring ability

Duroc: fast growers and efficient feeders; reddish in color with droopy ears

Hampshire: black with a white belt that extends from one front leg, over the shoulder, and down the other front leg; erect ears and known for lean, meaty carcasses

Poland China: six white points on a black body, similar to the Berkshire; medium-sized droopy ears

Spot: white with black spot, and medium-sized droopy ears; produces pigs with high growth rate

White Breeds:

Chester white: solid white, medium-sized droopy ears; good mothers that produce large litters; boars are usually aggressive

Landrance: good mothers with large, floppy ears and long bodies; highest weaned and post-weaning survival rate

Yorkshire: most sought-after breed; good mothers with long, large frames and white, erect ears

A SMALL FLOCK OF EWES provides wool. The addition of a ram provides lambs for sale.

Sheep

Wooly sheep racing across a pasture in a tight huddle is quite a scene. They travel in a clan, their crimped coats in natural and black, white and tawny brown, and combinations of all these. Crafters card and spin their own yard from the fine wool of shorn sheep, and some ethnic communities have traditions that include sheep meat. Hobby farmers with a bit of land can affordably start a small flock of ewes, which do their fair share of work in terms of pasture management.

Breeds

Currently, there are 47 breeds of sheep being raised in the United States. They are categorized by their coats and by their ability to produce meat and milk. Dual-breeds excel in both departments. Before deciding on a breed, consider your climate and select an animal with wool density that correlates with your weather. If you live in a northern region, choose sheep with some extra "lining" in their coats. On the other hand, fine wool and hair sheep are found in temperate and arid climates, respectively. Hair sheep do not require shearing, as they naturally shed their coats throughout the year. Fine-wool sheep produce baby-soft coats that are spun into merino yarns for making luxurious sweaters.

A HUDDLE of sheep travel in a close-knit pack.

SHEEP ARE SHORN IN THE SPRING every year, before the weather heats up.

ELECTRIC SHEARS make quick work of the sheep-shearing ritual.

Following are some categories of sheep you may consider:

Fine wool: known for their soft yarns; found in arid and semiarid regions, including Australia, South Africa, South America, and the western United States

Long wool: long-staple, lustrous crimped fleeces; found in cool rainy areas, such as England and Scotland. Border Leicester fleeces are sought after by people who spin wool into yarn

Dual-purpose: breeds produce good market lambs and yield quality wool fleeces; there are eight common dual-purpose breeds, including the Corriedale.

Hair sheep: do not produce wool, as their coats shed naturally; raised for meat and found in temperate climates

Meat breeds: raised exclusively for their meat; fat-tailed breeds store large amounts of fat in the rump area and are also raised for milk production

Minor: rare and less common breeds include the Jacob, which is small and multihorned with black spots and black facial markings over each eye.

Beware of Predators

According to a 2004 study by the National Agricultural Statistics Service, American sheep producers lost an estimated 614 sheep per day because of predators.

If you truly want to learn what yarn spinners desire in a wool and how to spot deficiencies as you shear, then learn how to spin. You'll soon find out why a yarn maker's pet peeves are excess vegetation and "second cuts," which are short pieces that are not as easily drafted and fed into a spinning wheel.

Sheep Care

Sheep need a sturdy fence and some type of shelter, though existing buildings on your land will suit them just fine. They are easy targets for predators, such as coyotes, so make certain your woven-wire pasture fence has a secure closure. Under stress, flighty sheep will get in a tizzy and scatter in a tight flock like a clique of teenage girls. Manage them more easily by building captures in the confined sheep area.

Sheep return your affection, and some ewes are prolific mothers. You can quickly multiply a herd with the help of a ram. (Or, pay a breeding fee rather than investing in a male.)

When purchasing sheep, look for healthy feet. From the front view, legs and hooves should align, as opposed to being knock-kneed, splayfooted, or pigeon-toed. Check the animal's bite, and be sure there are no udder lumps or skin lesions. Muddy trails on hind legs are a sign of diarrhea, which could indicate more serious health issues. Other poor health signs include runny nose, pale gums, mucus in the ears or eyes. Ask a vet to perform blood tests and a general exam before you take home a sheep. You do not want to introduce health problems to the rest of your flock by bringing home a sick sheep.

Fine Wool

Meat and wool are marketable products that sheep produce. While your intentions may only be to raise furry pets, unless they are hair sheep you will need to shear them, so you might as well aim to produce the cleanest, most desirable fleeces possible.

Caring for a sheep's coat involves the same rules humans follow for proper skin care. Good nutrition, plenty of sleep, and proper grooming habits will do more for your appearance than an expensive bottle of face cream. Similarly, a sheep's coat is a direct reflection of its environment. Good nutrition, well-managed pastures, parasite control, and vaccinations will ensure optimum health. In turn, its coat will grow lustrous, long, and thick: ideal for spinning wool into yarn.

A FABRIC COAT keeps fleece clean and dry, resulting in high-grade wool.

Some sheep farmers who are committed to producing quality fleeces for yarn spinners will actually outfit their sheep in special, fabric coats. These allow wool to breathe, but protect it from gathering vegetation, such as alfalfa feed that inevitably ends up getting tangled in their crimped coats. You can simply keep their shelter clean, and use straw bedding rather than wood chips, which are difficult to remove from fleeces after shearing. Do not allow the pasture to turn into a mud bowl. Practice managed intensive grazing (see page 132), and supplement their diet with alfalfa and grain if necessary.

GOATS ARE HIGH-SPIRITED ANIMALS that inject plenty of fun onto a farm. They'll maintain a pasture and produce dairy and a meal.

Goats

Goats are capable of all sorts of mischief. They're class clowns and escape artists with plenty of tricks for forcing through a fence if you provide them the opportunity. But their boundless energy and lovable nature make them a popular animal pick. Besides, they love to dine on the type of brush you want to clear: multiflora, leafy spurge, and kudzu. There are other reasons why hobby farmers are taking goats more seriously today. Besides adding character to your barn bunch, goats are prized for their protein-rich, lean chevon (meat), which is now a hot livestock niche market. Meanwhile, angora goats produce expensive luxury fiber that is spun into mohair.

Goat Care

Goats do not require a vast amount of resources, food, or shelter. They are ruminants that enjoy munching on twigs and leafy brush. In a pasture, they will consume one-sixth the amount of hay that a cow or horse will. However, if you raise milking goats, feed them with a forage of hay and grain to preserve the taste of the milk.

There is no need to build a fancy house for goats, as they fare well in dry, draft-free quarters. Goats are prone to respiratory problems triggered by a moist environment, so avoid heating that can result in condensation. House them in a three-sided barn, shed, or a shared barn with other animals. Invest your savings on shelter in quality fencing. Woven-wire pasture fencing is ideal, and additional strands of barbed or electrical wire will discourage curious goats and their kids from escaping.

A BOER GOAT rests in a stall with hay, which is typical bedding for most animals.

THIS ANGORA GOAT poses for a beauty shot. Imagine this curly frock transformed into a luxury garment. (It will first go through carding, processing, and spinning into yarn.)

Meat Goats

There is greater demand for chevon in the United States than there are farmers to supply the delicacy. In some cultures, goat meat is served as a main dish at weddings and religious celebrations and as daily fare, when available. Goat meat is prominent in dishes of Hispanic, Caribbean, Mediterranean, Eastern European, African, Middle Eastern, and Southeast Asian origin. As a hobby farm or large estate owner, your goals for land may not have initially included producing meat for sale. But if you decide to foray into agripreneurship, goat meat is a promising niche market.

Common meat goat breeds include the Spanish, myotonic, Nubian, Boer, and kiko. While many breeds of goats are raised for meat in other parts of the world, these specific goat meat breeds are leaner and more muscular. The myotonic breed is indigenous to the United States. It is termed wooden leg or stiff leg because these goats tend to lock their knees when excited or frightened, fall over, and lie stiff (faint) for 10 to 20 seconds. This quality comes from a recessive gene, so is usually not found in crossbred goats. Do your homework before purchasing a meat goat, and as with any animal breed, start with a small herd.

Angora Goats

These gentle creatures are mass-producers of luxury fiber. The demand for diamond fiber, as mohair is known, is strong; and angora goats can deliver. They yield 20 to 25 percent of their body weight in mohair fiber each year and are shorn in spring and fall. Crossbred angora goats produce different fiber colors, swaying from traditional white.

Caring for Angora goats requires attention to feeding, as their coats reflect diet content. They need quality pasture or hay and various protein rations during and after pregnancy. Serve Angora goats fresh, clean water. Stick to a regular parasite prevention program (deworming); lice is a threat to Angora goats. A pour-on product after shearing will prevent lice and ticks.

Q&A

Q: What is the difference between mohair and Angora fiber?

A: Angora goats produce fiber called mohair, while rabbits produce fiber called Angora. The nomenclature is confusing, but just remember: goats make mohair, rabbits yield Angora.

A YOUNGSTER learns responsibility by caring for animals, such as this calf.

Cattle

A pet cow is a generous companion who can supply you with milk, mow your pasture, and even help you pull a cart full of freshly picked produce. You don't need a range to raise a few cattle; certain miniatures and Jerseys are well suited for small acreage. Cows are peaceful roamers, when trained, and they keep good company with other animals in a barn.

Bovine Vocabulary

Calf: newborn cattle

Heifer: young female cattle

Cow: mature female cattle

Steer: castrated male cattle

Bull: young or mature male cattle (not castrated)

Polled: cattle that naturally does not have horns

Your Pet Cow

Do you want your cow to be purely a companion animal, or will you assign it a job like producing milk? You can adopt a cow to ride as you would a horse or choose a breed that likes to browse and munch away on brush, assisting in your land-clearing efforts. Many hobby farmers want a cow they can milk, so a Guernsey makes sense. Also, if you're looking for a family cow that will help fill your cooler with dairy, a Jersey is the fit for you. Let's not forget fertilizer—cows are prolific in the manure department.

Similar to sheep, you'll want to choose a cow that makes sense for your climate. Cattle wear their coats year-round, and certain breeds, such as Highlands, will not enjoy Georgia heat with their extra insulations, in the form of thick, shaggy hair. Talk to a veterinarian before you bring home a bovine, and find out what breeds best fit your lifestyle.

There are miniatures and cattle that don't mind a compact pasture, including Jerseys and dexters. You can ride a longhorn steer, and steers also perform better at pulling carts. You'll probably avoid bulls, which are temperamental. If you want your heifer to reproduce, you can always artificially inseminate her. Each breed requires different feed, so talk to your veterinarian or a county extension agent. If you will milk your cow, it will need more nutrition than what it finds rummaging through your pasture.

A Home for Cattle

Beef cattle can roam freely, but provide your pet cow with a home in a barn or a basic three-sided shelter. Fence in your pasture with cattle panels, wire mesh, or barbed wire. Use at least five strands. High-tensile electric fencing will prevent curious cattle from squeezing in between smooth wires. Your fence height and construction will depend on the size of animal you bring home. Miniatures will not need a 6-foot (1.8-m) barrier, but if you are training a mature steer, a tall enclosure is a good idea.

Caring for Cattle

If you've ever watched a cow rubbing against a fence, swatting its back with the whip of its tail, fretting and fussing, the culprit is most likely a fly. Horn flies and stable flies are two common cattle biters. Horn flies gather at the backs and sides of cows, and stable flies swarm around the legs. But gnats, horse flies, black flies, and deer flies also pester cattle. Their best defense is an insecticide product: oral larvacides, pour-on products, sprays, and insecticide-laced ear tags.

4-H Clubs

4-H clubs are a common pastime for youth who live in rural areas. This young boy cares for a baby chick.

A healthy cow has clean hooves and a coat free of mud and debris. These chores are up to you. Mud and manure-caked hooves can invite foot rot. You can prevent this by keeping your pasture from turning into a mud bowl and ensuring that the cow's shelter is clean, free of manure. Yes, you'll need to deal with all the mud piles in the pasture, too. You can compost the nitrogen-rich material and use it to fertilize turf—sustainability at work.

Bucket Calves

Bucket calves are newborns that are fed from a bottle or bucket with a nipple attached. They quickly develop a maternal attachment to the person who feeds it. Bucket calves are a great way to involve your children in animal-raising activities. They can learn responsibility and grow more comfortable handling and caring for other pet farm animals.

THIS LOP BUNNY enjoys a romp in the yard.

Rabbits

On the farm, rabbits are wool producers as well as cuddly companions. They require little real estate. They're small enough to cradle in your arms and petite enough to house in an economical hutch rather than a big barn. Children can learn animal care responsibilities with rabbits as pets. Cottontail bunnies, lop-eared rabbits, hares, take your pick. The rabbit world is full of different furry characters.

Ready for a Rabbit?

There are upwards of 50 different rabbit breeds, ranging from compact and slender hoppers to wooly types.

Lop bunnies come in different varieties, including the English lop with its long, droopy ears, and the American fuzzy lop, which weighs about 4 pounds (1.8 kg) when mature and has a round ball of a face with ears that hang down close to its cheeks. Depending on the breed, rabbits can weigh from 3 to 16 pounds (1.4 to 7.2 kg) when mature. Talk to a veterinarian before bringing home a rabbit to find out what type is appropriate for your family. You can find additional breeding information through the American Rabbit Breeders Association at www.arba.net.

Rabbit Care

Rabbits are herbivores that enjoy grains, greens, and hay. You can also purchase commercial rabbit pellets that are packed with essential nutrients. This is a convenient option, and you won't worry about whether rabbits are getting their vitamins. Pregnant does and does with litters require more nutrients, although you must be careful not to overfeed them. Obesity compacts internal organs, causing pregnancy complications. (This is true with most animals.) Serve rabbit meals in feed crocks, hoppers, or hay mangers. An automatic watering system will ensure a good, clean drink, though you can also use a crock.

Angora Rabbits

The fluffy white fur coat on Angora rabbits buries these bunnies in a soft cloud. Their wool is sought by hand spinners and those who appreciate knitting with the fine luxury fiber. Angora is often blended with other materials, including sheep's wool, mohair (from Angora goats), and silk. Angora wool is sheared or plucked.

There are four major Angora breeds recognized by the Angora Rabbit Breeders Association. Those are English, French, satin, and giant. Giant Angoras are 9½ pounds (4.3 kg) or larger, and they are efficient wool producers. English Angoras are petite in comparison, at 5 to 7½ pounds (2.3 to 3.4 kg). Their wooly faces and ears give them a teddy bear look, so they are often chosen as pet breeds. Before deciding, talk to other Angora owners and learn the merits.

Nest Boxes

BEFORE A DOE HAS KITS (baby rabbits), prepare a nest box so she can separate herself from the herd. This nest box will serve as a safe zone for mom and a nursing area once kits are born. Set the nest box in the hutch about 28 days after breeding.

BUNNIES ARE NICE starter animals if you want to test the waters before moving on to larger responsibilities, such as cows or sheep.

THIS BASIC RABBIT HUTCH is easy to build from cedar.

Rabbit Hutches

Rabbits live in compact wire hutches that are about 2 feet (61 cm) high and about 2½ feet (76.2 cm) deep. Length depends on the breed. Small rabbits can live in a 3-foot (91.4-cm) hutch. Allow 4 feet (1.2 m) for medium rabbits and 6 feet (1.8 m) for large breeds.

This rabbit hutch is an easy-to-build outdoor shelter for your bunny. The floor is made of hardware cloth which allows droppings to fall through but is easy on the rabbit's feet. A large airy compartment is enclosed with hardware cloth and a cozy smaller compartment is sided for warmth and privacy/safety. Each compartment has a door to make feeding and cage cleaning an easier task.

Place straw or wood shavings in the compartment to make comfortable bedding for the bunny.

Finish the rabbit hutch with an animal-safe exterior stain. Place the hutch in a protected area out of direct sun.

OVERALL SIZE:

54" HIGH

32" WIDE

48" LONG

TOOLS & MATERIALS

- **2 × 2 × 6' cedar (7)**
- **2 × 4" × 6' cedar (7)**
- **¾" fence staples**
- **⅝" × 4 × 8' grooved cedar plywood siding**
- **1 ¼" and 2 ½" deck screws**
- **3 × 3" hinges (4)**
- **hook and eye fasteners (4)**
- **½" × 4 × 8' hardware cloth**

How to Build a Rabbit Hutch

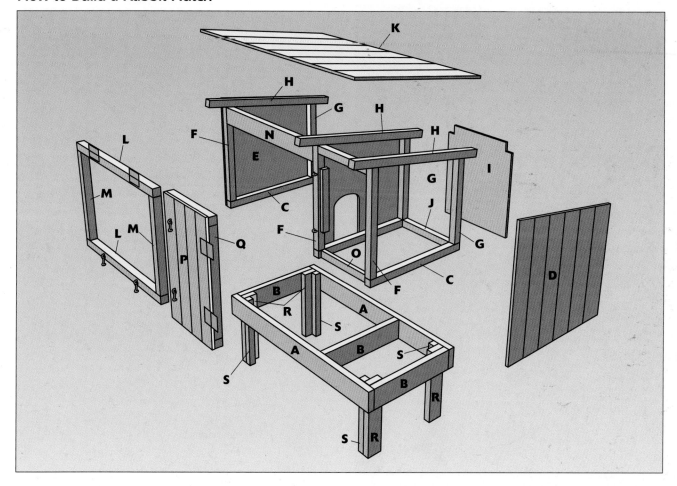

Cutting List

Key	Part	Dimension	Pcs.	Material		Key	Part	Dimension	Pcs.	Material
A	Floor side	1½ × 3½ × 47½"	2	Cedar		K	Roof	½ × 32 × 48"	1	Siding
B	Floor crosspiece	1½ × 3½ × 21"	3	Cedar		L	Door crosspiece	½ × 1½ × 29½"*	2	Cedar
C	Frame base	1½ × 1½ × 24"	3	Cedar		M	Door side	1½ × 1½ × 17½"*	2	Cedar
D	Right side wall	½ × 24 × 24"	1	Siding		N	Hinge support	1½ × 3½ × 29½"*	1	Cedar
E	Left side wall	½ × 24 x 24"	1	Siding		O	Door jamb	1½ × 1½ × 13¼"*	1	Cedar
F	Frame front	1½ × 1½ × 21"*	3	Cedar		P	Compartment door	½ × 13 × 22½"*	1	Siding
G	Frame back	1½ × 1½ × 17½"*	3	Cedar		Q	Door supports	1½ × 1½ × *	4	Cedar
H	Frame top	1½ × 1½ × 32"	3	Cedar		R	Legs	1½ × 3½ × *	4	Cedar
I	Back wall	½ × 17¼ × 20"	1	Siding		S	Legs	1½ × 1½ × *	4	Cedar
J	Back wall stop	1½ × 1½ × 13¼"	1	Siding						

*cut to fit

Note: Measurements reflect the actual size of dimension lumber.

A SWARM OF BEES cling to foliage that is sweet with pollen.

Beekeeping

Harvest fresh sweetener for teas, cakes, and toast from beehives kept in your own backyard. Honey is a long-time folk medicine packed with antioxidants and purported to heal wounds. The "liquid gold" was traded in Greek and Roman times, and today we covet the sticky, amber-colored fluid mainly for culinary purposes. Raising bees has its minor risks—a sting from time to time and perhaps some angry neighbors if you don't watch where you place hives. But you can start a hive of honeybees in a small space with little capital. All you need is a semi-secluded plot where flowers bloom.

Get Started

Before you delve into the business of raising honeybees, be sure your county does not require permits or licenses. If your property is located in a more developed area, there may be limits to the number of hives you can own.

Order everything you need to start a hive from a bee supplier, including the bees, which are shipped via mail. The intricacies of beekeeping are best learned from experienced beekeepers. Learn more from the American Beekeeping Federation, and seek out a local bee club to meet others who pursue the hobby.

Hive Basics

The backbone of a hive is constructed from frames made of beeswax comb. A Langstroth hive is the most common and efficient hive construction. It opens at the top and has movable frames, allowing "bee space" between each for bees to build their combs. Bee space is the crawl space where bees pass through the hive. If the bee space is too small, the bee will seal it with propolis. This means no honey. If the space allows more room than the bee needs to pass through, it will build a comb. Those combs contain the honey product you will harvest from the hive by removing the frames.

Did You Know?
Honeybees are vegetarians that crave pollen, which provides necessary protein and carbohydrates. **Yellow jackets** feed mostly on scavenged meat and insects.

Bee colonies can help pollinate crops and flowers. Over time, a flower garden where bees populate and gather food will produce larger, vibrant blooms. Some farmers will rent bee colonies, usually two per acre, to pollinate their orchards and field crops at the beginning of the bloom.

THE LANGSTROTH hive features stackable frames with plenty of "bee space" where combs are formed.

Bee Supplies

Clothing: bee veil, a bee suit or white coveralls (bees don't like dark colors), work boots, bee gloves

Tools: bee smoker, hive tool, electric uncapping knife, honey extractor, honey storage tank

Hive: brood chambers, honey supers, queen excluder to keep the queen from laying eggs in honey supers, hive cover, hive stand to improve air circulation

Note: hive bodies hold nine or ten frames and a foundation. Each frame contains a sheet of beeswax or a plastic foundation. Bees build cells of secreted wax on these frames.

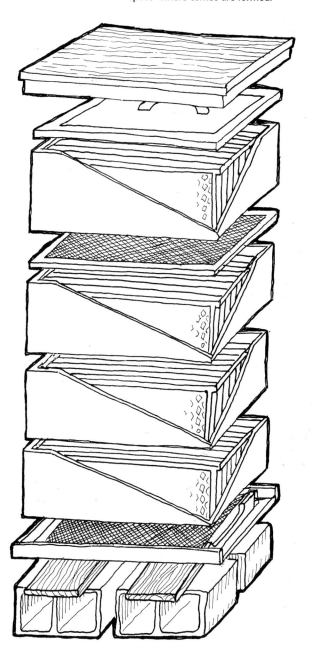

Alpaca

Lock eyes with a quizzical alpaca and you'll feel like you are being probed for information, as if the animal is trying to get to know you. The alpaca hums peacefully, occasionally clicking or clucking a message to its babies. Topped with fluffy Mohawks of touchable fiber, alpacas are shorn annually. They grow thick coats that are five times warmer than wool and far more durable. Yarn spinners covet alpaca fiber, farmers admire these loving pets, and investors appreciate the tax advantages and potential returns these valuable creatures promise.

About Alpacas

Alpacas are members of the camelid family, smaller cousins to their relatives llamas and camels. Their value as a pet and producer of fine fiber dates back to the Incan culture of South America; the first alpacas were imported to the United States in 1984. Alpacas are an approachable livestock, which makes them appealing to landowners who want to begin caring for animals. They won't challenge your fencing or trample your pasture (their feet are padded). They require little feed, eating only about 2 pounds (.9 kg) of food per 125 pounds (56 kg) of body weight per day. So, an average 60-pound (27 kg) bale of hay can feed 20 alpacas for a day. Compare this to sheep, that eat about 6 pounds (2.7 kg) of food per day.

Alpacas grow to an average height of 36 inches (91.4 cm) at the withers, and they weigh between 100 and 175 pounds (45 to 78.8 kg). Up to ten alpacas can graze on an acre of pasture, which makes them ideal small-farm animals. Most alpaca farms are less than 10 acres in size, and owners generally start with a small herd of three to five females.

A CURIOUS ALPACA peeks through its fence. An alpaca's gestation period is nearly one year for a single cria (baby) like this one pictured.

THE OLD SAYING, "You are what you eat" applies equally to animals. This alpaca munches on quality hay from a specialized feeder.

Preparing a Home

The fencing you'll build for an alpaca farm is designed more to keep predators out than to keep alpacas in. Alpacas are generally not ambitious escape artists—not nearly as tricky as goats. But coyotes, and even your farm dog, can represent a threat to sensitive alpacas. Alpacas indicate they are in danger by making a shrill bugling sound, which is a dramatic change from their usual hum. Install perimeter, no-climb fencing that is at least 5 feet (1.5 m) tall. Separate females and males with fencing, and females and their newborn crias must have separate quarters. However, do not completely isolate them from the group. Alpacas are herd animals.

A three-sided shelter is adequate for alpacas, which are accustomed to rugged, cold climates. Heat is more of a concern, and their insulating fiber coats are no help in keeping them cool in summer. A misting system or fans in the alpaca shelter will prevent them from overheating.

Fiber

Alpaca fiber is stronger, lighter, and softer than wool. It grows in 22 basic colors with many variations and blends. Breeders who raise alpacas to sell fiber—and there aren't many in the United States who depend solely on this industry for income—experiment with breeding combinations to produce attractive colors and

pay close attention to feed. Alpacas bred for fiber will not obtain all necessary nutrients from pasture grazing.

Spinning, dyeing, and selling fiber has become a cottage industry for some who raise alpacas. The Alpaca Fiber Cooperative of North America (AFCNA) was founded to raise awareness and demand for fiber in the United States. The AFCNA serves as an outlet for alpaca owners who want to send their fiber to the association for processing and distribution.

Did You Know?

Alpacas are known for a rather offensive defense mechanism: spitting. They normally do not spit at people, unless you interfere in a squabble or are perceived as an intruder. Alpacas can be taught not to spit at people just as dogs can be trained to sit and stay. However, in the pasture a swift spit from a "king" alpaca lets others sharing the space know who's boss.

Llamas are roughly twice the size of alpacas, and they are often used as guard animals to prevent predators from entering alpaca territory.

ALPACAS have one of the longest gestation periods of any farm animal: almost a year.

Breeding

Female alpacas can give birth to one baby, called a cria, each year. Their gestation period is 11½ months. Alpacas generally give birth during daylight hours, thanks to their cold-climate roots. Crias usually weigh between 15 and 20 pounds (6.8 and 9 kg) and, if healthy, crias can be up on their feet within an hour. After four to six months, crias are weaned from their mothers. Female alpacas (dams) are ready to breed once they reach 75 percent of their adult weight, which is usually between one and two years after birth.

The majority of alpacas in the United States are registered with the Alpaca Registry Inc. (ARI), which is the largest alpaca pedigree register in the world. Crias are DNA tested to validate that parents are also registered. Upon validation, the ARI provides a certificate that describes known lineage back to the point of importation. Each alpaca is assigned a unique number. This process of registration is valuable to alpaca owners who invest in these expensive creatures to ensure they are buying what they think they are buying. In many ways, registration is an insurance policy.

Investment Opportunities

Most people who are considering alpacas want to know about the talked-about investment opportunities these animals afford. What about those tax write-offs? Alpacas cost how much?

Alpacas have always been valuable creatures, historically for their fiber and today because of a breeding demand and limited supply in the United States. The price of a female alpaca can range from $10,000 to $40,000 (or less, depending on the color, fiber, lineage, etc.). Males range from $5,000 to $35,000 and in excess of $200,000 for proven studs. Some owners raise only females and pay breeding fees for winning studs in hopes of improving their herd. Their goals, in essence, are to achieve superior, crimped fiber (the more crimped and thick, the better yarn it produces); to breed alpacas in colors that are appealing to buyers (black and brown variations are generally more popular than white); and to raise alpacas to show, win awards, and therefore add value to their herd.

Alpacas are in hot demand, and because of their slow growth as a population they hold their value as a long-term investment that can earn you income and offer tax advantages. Female alpacas can give birth to no more than one cria each year. The United States no longer allows imports of alpacas from countries such as South America. Artificial insemination is virtually impossible because of alpacas' physical characteristics. Finally, virtually every U.S. alpaca is registered with the Alpaca Registry Inc., so you can maintain a certificate that describes lineage.

FOR FUN OR FOR SHOW, raising and riding horses is perhaps the biggest reason behind the recent growth in the number of hobby farms.

Horses

Imagine the rhythmic clip-clop of your horse's hooves as you explore trails on your property—a smooth gait as you glide through open acres. For many people who acquire a bit of land, a horse is the next purchase after the property deal is signed and sealed. While horses will work hard on a farm if trained and their promise as an investment is appealing to some, your main purpose for owning horses will probably be for the pure joy of riding.

If you are a novice equestrian who seeks a horse purely for pleasure riding, then you should carefully evaluate a horse's disposition, soundness, and trainability. You want a horse that is a comfortable height and width so you can straddle it without struggling and ride it with ease. The horse should have a mild temperament so the whole family can approach, ride, and care for it.

Soundness refers to a horse's ability to perform ex-

pected activities. It includes vision, breathing, and athleticism. A mature trained horse is best for beginner and young riders. Choose a healthy horse (with the help of an equine veterinarian) that you connect with personally. Recreation horses are pets, after all.

If you simply want to own the horse and plan to turn its care over to a professional, then don't select a horse without an experienced adviser. Also, understand that earning a decent income from horses is a full-time job, and horse investments are risky. Success requires a lot of luck, a horse with credentials like gold, and deep knowledge of the horse business. We could not possibly delve into the intricacies of race horses, breeding, or showing in this chapter. Instead, consider this a 101 course on how to make a comfortable home for a horse and how to pick the right horse for your needs.

Horses used for pleasure and trail riding do not need to be registered. If you want to breed horses, only invest in a registered horse with certification that will detail its lineage.

Acquiring Your Horse

Mares and geldings (castrated males) have agreeable temperaments for pleasure and trail riding. You may be attracted to a beautiful mare, but her attitude will change drastically when she's in season. Stallions should be reserved only for breeders and experienced handlers. Instead, beginners should seek a horse that is already trained and has settled down a bit. It may seem that a young child should have a young horse, but this logic is way off base. Mature horses make great riding pets. Because horses live to be as old as 30, you'll get plenty of years of companionship and riding, even if you bring it home after its 10th birthday. While you can invest in a younger horse, you'll need the services of a professional trainer, and it could be years before the horse is ready to take a slow, easy ride.

Where do you find a horse that's ready to ride? First, understand that all horses will require a bit of training from you, its new owner. It's a good idea to sign up for classes or work with an experienced horseman as you get to know your horse. You can purchase horses from dealers, public auctions, horse farm sales, and rescue foundations. You may also find an owner who wants to sell a horse that a rider has outgrown, or perhaps they have lost interest in the hobby. On all accounts, buyer beware. Your best bet is to consult with an equine veterinarian to be sure the horse you are considering for purchase is healthy and sound. Also, ask the seller for a warranty.

A VETERINARIAN examines this pregnant mare.

THIS ROOMY STABLE is home to several horses. The structure receives adequate ventilation through its open sides, which close in inclimate weather.

A Home for Your Horse

Horses require a comfortable shelter that is free of drafts, dampness, and condensation. Each horse should have a private stall with a window to let in sunlight and fresh air. Ideally, your barn will also include a feed room, storage for hay and bedding, and a tack room. A clean, dry barn provides a healthy environment for horses, and the first of these two requirements is your responsibility. You should muck the stalls daily. This involves cleaning manure from the living space with a pitchfork with closely spaced tines. (You'll also need a broom, plastic bucket, and a good attitude—remember, this dirty job is for the sake of your horse's health!)

If you're starting from scratch with a barn, check into the modular kits available today. You can quickly assemble a sound structure for your horse without the labor or cost of raising a good old-fashioned barn. Prefabricated barn kits are especially ideal for homeowners who have a couple of acres and close neighbors.

Avoid cement floors in your barn, which are hard on horses' joints. A clay surface free of rocks, covered with clean bedding, such as straw, is the ideal barn floor for horses. Be sure there is ample lighting in your stable, and control rodents and pests as necessary. (Barn owls work wonders.) Horses are comfortable in 32 degree Fahrenheit weather (0 degrees Celsius), but you may outfit them with a blanket or heat the barn. Just be sure the barn is adequately ventilated so condensation doesn't build up, which can trigger respiratory problems.

Fence in your stable area and allow a minimum of 800 square feet (74.3 sq. m) for an exercise area. Avoid barbed wire fencing, which can cause injury if a horse is spooked and makes a run for the exit. Wood, metal, and electric fencing will contain horses. However, if you choose electric fencing to divide a pasture, be sure to train the horses so they do not harm themselves out of ignorance.

Your pasture will likely serve as a horse workout area, not a feeding zone. Though horses are fine grazers, they prefer pastures with dense forage, which requires high-fertility soil and quite a bit of maintenance. You'll probably choose to feed horses a balanced ration of protein, energy, vitamins, and minerals through a commercial feed and hay combination. This way, you can assure they are receiving proper nutrition. Before relying on your pasture for feed, consult with a county extension agent and determine how you can fortify your pasture to serve horses' needs.

DILIGENT HOOF CARE will prevent disease. Clean horse hooves daily, scraping manure and caked mud from their feet. Also, freshen the bedding and regularly muck the stalls.

Farm Dogs

Your farm dog may be a lazy basset hound that is more interested in guarding the refrigerator than your sheep or an ambitious border collie that will herd your livestock in from the pasture each night. Some dogs work on farms, but they all embrace the land as their personal theme park. There's room to roam, sniff, root around, chase furry animals, and paw around in a mess of outdoor treats, including the kind from your pasture that you don't want tracked into your home. Dogs are naturals on the farm. Choose a pet to be your right-hand helper, and train it so it stays safe on your land.

Herding Breeds

Certain dog breeds are naturals at herding sheep, protecting cattle, and working as canine security guards. Herding breeds are obedient and can be trained to perform herding tasks on your farm. They are gentle workers, but show gumption and strength in their ability to face up to stubborn animals. Herding dogs cooperate with their handlers while using their own initiative to get the job done.

There are herding organizations and training classes for dogs, and these groups will also be a valuable resource as you decide what dog is a best fit for your farm. Some common herd breeds include German and Australian shepherds, Shetland sheepdogs, collies, Pembroke Welsh corgies, Australian cattle dogs, and Old English sheepdogs.

ON THE FARM, dogs are constant companions that perform a variety of important jobs.

A FARM IS A TRUE PLAYGROUND for your family dogs. If they are well trained, they will keep themselves out of trouble (for the most part), but fencing in your property is always a good idea if you own animals.

Basic Training

Your companion dog must learn some ground rules on your hobby farm. Your neighbors may be a mile away or within eyeshot of your front porch. Fencing is a great idea in a big backyard, and it's essential on multiple acres, especially if you raise livestock. A sturdy fence will prevent your dog from running onto country roads, which may not be as busy, but with high speed limits the trucks that barrel down those byways are not forgiving. A fence will also ensure that your pooch doesn't wander to the neighbors' properties, harass their sheep, bark at their horses, or scare their prized goat into a fainting spell.

Fencing within your property will keep dogs out of pastures where your animals graze. A roaming dog among active horses is liable to get a swift kick in the face.

Teach your dog basic training commands: sit, stay, come, leave it. You may not be able to command your dog to run into the house and fetch you a cool glass of water, but you can prevent disasters like running into streets, pastures, and other no-dog zones. All that land is doggy heaven—your pup doesn't need to run free to enjoy your great outdoors.

Appendix

In Case of Emergency

A number of factors will slow emergency response time in rural environments. For one, your home is likely miles away from the nearest fire and police departments. Their territories are widespread, so resources must cover lots of ground. Then, even if help is dispatched within minutes of your call, your disaster may escalate beyond control before resources arrive. There are floods, tornadoes, and other acts of nature. You can't control the weather, but you certainly can prepare for it. The equipment you use on a daily basis poses risk. There are measures you can take on all accounts to ensure the safety of your family and animals. The key is to develop a grand disaster management plan.

Prepare with a Plan

Start with the house and work your way out to the barn, shed, yard, fields, and surrounding landscape that may present risks of wildfire or flooding. Jot down notes as you consider potential risks in each of these areas. Develop two escape routes (one main and one backup) for each room in your home and barn. Finally, how will you exit your property? If a rescue team needs to reach your property, what is the best way for them to find you? Keep emergency phone numbers handy, and communicate this information with your family. Also, go through the home together and identify all power switches and gas and water line shutoffs.

STANDBY POWER IS ESSENTIAL on a working farm. A diesel-powered standby generator is best. You may want to have separate generators for your farmhouse and your barn.

IT'S WISE to adopt a no-smoking policy for your barn.

In the barn or shed, take similar notes: identify electrical outlets; power, water, and gas line switches (if applicable); and two possible exits in case of emergency. If you have animals, have you constructed a fenced-in area outside the barn so they can escape on their own? How will you transport them away from danger, and where will they go? (See Evacuating Animals on page 170.) Be sure that your barn and shed are equipped with fire extinguishers and smoke detectors. Barns may also have sprinkler systems.

In the yard or field, how will you call for help if an accident happens on a piece of machinery or if you suffer a work injury unexpectedly? Consider carrying a cell phone with you in case you need to call for assistance and you're stranded acres away from the house. (Whomever is inside may not hear your cries for help.)

A key part of disaster preparation is paperwork: property insurance, flood insurance, life and health insurance. In extreme circumstances when insurance will not cover damaged property or economic injury, the USDA Farm Service Agency provides some low-interest loans. Learn all you can about potential risks on your property posed by climate, topography, or weather trends. Talk to local enforcement agents about problems that often arise in your area. Also, get to know the USDA's extension service, which offers information and materials concerning hazard prevention.

Prevent Barn Fires

Consider the contents of your shed or barn: equipment, hay, electrical devices, cleaning agents, fertilizers, power tools. Often, these structures become collection sites for odds and ends and who-knows-what. It's no wonder that barn fires are a common disaster in rural areas. Combine flammable materials (hay, fertilizer) with antiquated electrical outlets or running equipment, and you have the ingredients for fire. When animals are involved, the scenario becomes tragic. You may be forced to make a heartbreaking moral decision: save the livestock or yourself?

You can prevent barn and shed fires with a few simple measures. In a barn, never store wet hay, which can combust. High-moisture haystacks can produce chemical reactions that build heat. The more hay in the stack, the less cool air can penetrate and moderate the temperature. The lesson: Never store wet hay in your barn. Also, take care when starting equipment indoors, and be sure there is plenty of ventilation in the space. Fire extinguishers and smoke detectors are critical. Sensors that note changes in temperature will alert you of dangerous conditions before a fire occurs.

Equipment Safety

Whether you're operating a compact utility tractor on rocky terrain or a string trimmer on a manicured lawn, equipment can pose safety risks if not utilized according to instructions in operators' manuals. Always read the manufacturer's instructions before turning the ignition of your brand-new tractor or priming the two-cycle engine of a leaf blower. No exceptions.

The operators' manual will explain important safety messages. For instance, never operate mowing equipment with the discharge chute raised, removed, or altered, unless using a grass catcher. This device is designed to reduce the chance of thrown objects. Larger equipment, such as compact utility vehicles and skid steer loaders, are equipped with roll-over protection systems (ROPS). These roll bars should never be removed. They will prevent the machine from crushing you, should you tip the equipment during operation. Read instructions for running mowers and tractors on slopes and across rough land. In every case, use caution. And do not ignore suggestions to use eye or ear protection.

Flood Risk

The best protection against flooding is flood insurance, which is separate from property insurance. Talk to an insurance agent about obtaining a policy so you can protect your assets. You can obtain a flood insurance rate map (FIRM) online at the Federal Emergency Management Agency (FEMA) Center, www.fema.gov. For flood-control measures, such as minimizing runoff on your property, consult with an extension agent to discuss grading, culverts, and watersheds.

TALK TO YOUR SERVICING DEALER about potential hazards on your land and how to manage those while operating equipment.

Evacuating Animals
Your animals deserve a disaster plan.

Identification: Tag animals with some sort of identification to improve their chances of a safe return in case they make their own escape.

A Host: Establish evacuation sites for your animals—a neighbor or another host who can house your animals for a short time following an incident.

Transportation: Secure trailers and trucks required to transport animals from the disaster site to a safe zone.

The American Farmland Trust is a valuable resource for learning about land conservation and estate planning. Log on to www.farmland.org.

Protect Your Investment

What would happen to your land if you pitched a For Sale sign in the front yard today? Would your first bidder be a farmer or a developer?

The answer to this question depends largely on the amount of land you own and where your property is located. If your goal is to preserve the land for your heirs or at least sell it to someone who will maintain its integrity as a hobby farm and not "sell out" to developers, then you must prepare legal documents to protect your property.

Future Thinking

Perhaps you just purchased your property and have not even moved to your new home. Or maybe you've been working the land for years, whether that means mowing a great estate or plowing hay fields. While you can't imagine living anywhere else now, what will happen 10 or 20 years down the road? What if you've decided that the country life isn't for you, and you want out?

In any case, your first charge is to decide how you want the land to be used in the future. Is it important to you that the property is farmed and not developed? Do you want to preserve the woods or agricultural integrity? Would you sell a portion of your land to buyers who want to build homes on the land, then save the rest as farmland? Consider your intentions for the property.

Next, discuss the future of the land with your family and find out if there are interested heirs who want to be next in line. In some families, children who grow up on the land can't wait for the day they pack their bags and move to the city. Other families have owned property for generations and wish to continue the legacy. The legal arrangements you make for your land will depend on whether the next owners will be heirs or buyers.

IF YOU WANT YOUR HOBBY FARM to stay in your family after you move on, planning for that transition should be one of the first acts you take.

Acknowledgements

Kristen Hampshire is an award-winning writer and author of four outdoor design and landscaping books branded by John Deere, including John Deere's *Lawn Care & Landscaping* (Quayside 2007); *52 Backyard Projects: Design, Build and Plant the Yard of Your Dreams One Weekend at a Time* (Quayside 2008); and *Stonescaping Made Simple* (Creative Publishing International 2009). Hampshire has been published in *Ladies' Home Journal*, *Fortune Small Business*, *Vogue Knitting*, *The Tennessean*, *Cleveland* magazine and *Cooking Light*.

A former editor for a landscape journal, Hampshire launched her business, WriteHand Co., in 2004. She specializes in home & garden and interior design and is a member of the American Society of Journalists and Authors (ASJA). Hampshire works and lives in Bay Village, Ohio, with her husband, Haven Ohly, and a curious scottie dog, Mayzie. Check out Hampshire's website at www.kristenhampshire.com.

Author Acknowledgements: My sincere appreciation goes to Daphne and Bob Borden, who generously opened their home to me and invited us to photograph their slice of paradise. Paynter Farm was a significant source of inspiration for many of the chapters in this book. Daphne, thank you for introducing me to a very special place (and for that delicious brown bread recipe, which is a treasure). Your land has a spirit all its own. Betsy Gammons, you made the connection—thank you. I so enjoyed the New England visit! (Don't think I've forgotten about that extra bedroom you mentioned...) To Rosalind Wanke, for your direction and expertise during the photo shoot at Paynter Farm, and Eric Roth, for capturing the energy there.

Back in Ohio, Cheryl and Albert Laufer of Spirit Wind Alpacas in Newbury, put me to work at their annual shearing. I'm still amazed at the speed of those humming trimmers and the stacks of luscious fiber. Cheryl, we met at a writers' conference, discovered a common love of fiber, and I've enjoyed the trips to your farm since.

To Michael White for his time and interest in my work with this book. I see why you named that alpaca "BMW." He owns that title. And I enjoyed that tidbit about celebrating the barn raising with KFC and a bottle of champagne.

Sean Sundberg, I picked your brain quite a bit and you always made the time. Your expertise was valuable to this project.

Thank you Mark Johanson for your editorial direction, and Jenny Gehlhar for loving this book as much as I do. To the team at Creative Publishing International for ushering this book to completion: Jon Simpson, Michele Lanci-Altomare, and Val Escher.

At the homestead, I'm grateful for the support of my husband, Haven, and my family—mom, dad, Erik. And to my favorite girl and our newest addition, a Scottie named Mayzie. She could use a sheep friend, I think.

Resources

There is a bounty of resources to help you purchase, plan, build, grow, and develop your land. Start with your local county extension agency—an invaluable outlet for information pertaining to your land. Following is a laundry list of references for you to explore, from magazines to special-interest associations and government agencies.

Alpaca Fiber Cooperative of North America (AFCNA)
www.americasalpaca.com

Alpaca Owners and Breeders Association (AOBA)
www.alpacainfo.com

Alpaca Registry Inc.
www.alpacaregistry.net

Alternative Technology Transfer for Rural America (ATTRA)
www.attra.org; (800) 346-9140

American Farmland Trust
www.farmland.org

American Sheep Industry Association
www.sheepusa.org

American Rabbit Breeders Association
www.arba.net

Bee Source
www.beesource.com

Cattle Today
www.cattletoday.com

The Cornucopia Institute
www.cornucopia.org

Country Living Association
www.countrylivingassociation.org

Countryside magazine
www.countrysidemag.com

Federal Emergency Management Agency (FEMA)
www.fema.gov

Goat World
www.goatworld.com

Hobby Farms
www.hobbyfarms.com

Horse Channel
www.horsechannel.com

Iowa State University Extension
www.extension.iastate.edu

John Deere
www.johndeere.com

Land Trust Alliance
www.lta.org

Living the Country Life magazine
www.livingthecountrylife.com

National Angora Rabbit Breeders Club
www.nationalangorarabbitbreeders.com

The Nature Conservancy
www.nature.org

Ohio State University Extension
www.extension.osu.edu

Organic Crop Improvement Association (OCIA)
www.ocia.org; (402) 477-2323

Purdue University Extension
www.ces.purdue.edu

Successful Farming magazine
www.agriculture.com

Sustainable Agriculture Research and Education (SARE)
www.sare.org

U. S. Department of Agriculture. Living on an Acre: A Practical Guide to the Self-Reliant Life
Guilford, Connecticut: Thy Lyons Press, 2003.

USDA Economic Research Service
www.ers.usda.gov

USDA National Organic Program
www.ams.usda.gov/nop

Photography Credits

Robert Agli
p. 122, 162, 170

Janet Backhaus
p. 12 (lower right)

Belgard
p. 81

Bob Firth
p. 43 (top)

Kim Flottum
p. 158

Foxhill Farm Photography
Daniel Johnson: p. 39, 52, 53, 104, 120, 123, 126 (left), 131, 133, 138, 140 (top & lower right), 145, 148 (middle), 151 (both), 152, 164
Paulette Johnson: p. 4 (left), 14 (top), 26, 114, 119, 125 (top right), 126 (middle & right), 132, 134, 135, 141 (lower), 143, 144 (top & lower), 146 (top), 148 (lower, Shirley Fernandez/Paulette Johnson), 149, 153

Fuchs & Kasperek, Inc.
p. 7 (lower), 19

Generac Power Systems, Inc.
p. 168

GeoEye
www.geoeye.com
p. 37

Kristen Hampshire
p. 27, 36

Istock / www.istock.com
p. 4 (middle & right), 7 (top, Marissa Childs), 13 (lower, Alex Slobodkin), 13 (top, Matteo de Stefano), 14 (lower), 15 (lower left), 16 (lower, Stig Anderson; top, Simone Vanden-Berg), 18 (Jill Fromer), 20 (Barnabás Füzes), 21 (Gene Krebs), 24 (middle & right), 25, 32 (top left, Roger Whiteway; multiflora, Gabor Izso; briar, Lisa Thornberg; thistle, Alexander Todorenko; bittersweet, Amy Kimball; poison ivy, Chris Hill), 40, 41, 50 (Tatiana Boyle), 80, 82 (right), 92 (right top & lower), 93, 94, 98, 101, 118, 125 (top left & lower two), 128, 130, 136 (Craig Hanson), 137, 140 (lower left), 141 (top), 142, 150 (Eric van den Elsen), 154 (Sean Locke), 155, 159, 160, 161, 165 (top)

John Deere
p. 9, 60, 62–63, 66–67, 70 (all), 71 (right), 73 (top), 76, 78–79, 88, 107

Max-Flex Fence Systems
p. 43 (lower), 44 (left)

Donna Moratelli
p. 5, 12 (lower left), 42, 48, 58 (middle), 72, 73 (middle & lower), 92 (left), 137 (top), 139, 146 (lower)

Shelley Metcalf
p. 6, 121

Jerry Pavia
p. 30, 32 (multiflora wild rose bloom & purple loosestrife), 108, 113

Eric Roth
p. 10 (lower), 11 (top & lower), 12 (top), 15 (right), 17, 32 (lower), 34, 35, 51, 54, 58, 59, 64, 82 (left), 83, 96, 105, 115, 116, 126, 129, 147, 148 (top), 163, 165 (lower), 166, 167, 169

Beth Singer
p. 10 (top)

SMB Manufacturing, Inc.
p. 133 (top, automatic watering bowls)

Susan Teare
p. 58 (right), 61, 65, 171

Bryan Trandem
p. 124

Index